The Origin of Morgans

It was the quality of the craftsmanship which was inherent in the handsome design of the Swansea Harbour Trust building which attracted owners Martin and Louisa Morgan, when they set out to develop an exclusive hotel here in Swansea. The more they found out about the building, the more they realised that the design of the century-old structure matched their own perceptions of the kind of service which they wished to provide for their guests. Indeed, the Trust building seemed to them to be a statement of the ethos which they wished to develop. They had in their minds an environment of exceptional quality, matched by excellent service, provided in an atmosphere which reflected both of these things. And, in September 2002, following almost two years of painstaking planning and renovation, the building was given new life as Morgans. Happily, for Martin and Louisa, their perceptions, based largely upon the appeal of the outside of the structure, proved to closely match the design brief which was the basis for the construction of the original building. The old adage about classical design being timeless, being shown, yet again, to be valid.

The organisation called the Swansea Harbour Trust was established by an act of Parliament in 1791. The task of the trust was to 'enlarge and preserve the harbour of the town of Swansea in the county of Glamorganshire'. After a fitful start, in a burgeoning environment in which the industrialisation of south Wales proceeded at great pace, much was achieved by the body. By the end of the nineteenth century, the business of the trust had increased significantly. Indeed, such was the volume of business being transacted at that time that the trustees believed that they should erect a purpose-designed building which reflected the contribution of the trust to the economic well-being of the town of Swansea. The discussion upon which that decision was based proved to be the genesis for the construction of the handsome building which, today, is Morgans.

The next stage in the process involved the board of trustees developing, with professional advice, the design brief which reflected their operational and aesthetical requirements. It was that brief which was used as the basis for a design competition among potential architects and, from over one hundred entries, that submitted by Edwin Seward of Cardiff was selected and the process of construction begun. Seward was delighted to win the competition and to have the opportunity to work with a client organisation for whom only the best materials for the purpose were good enough. It followed that the material specifications both internal and external were of first quality, which allowed Seward and the building contractor, Lloyd Brothers of Swansea, to indulge themselves in their quest to build a magnificent facility for the Harbour Trust organisation. In addition, they were able to employ, directly or through subcontracting, the very best craftsmen available. When the building was opened on 12 October 1903, it was clear to all who attended the official ceremony, that the combination of effective design, superior quality materials and the work of talented craftsmen, had produced a superb, handsome construction which was an asset, not only to the Harbour Trust but to Swansea itself. To put this into context, it is interesting to note the words of the *Cambrian* reporter who covered the opening ceremony. He wrote:

> The new building has practically remodelled the whole appearance of this part of Swansea. The long expanse of red brick, diversified by bands of Portland stone strike a bright and pleasant

note amongst the surroundings which are distinctly dingy by comparison.

In his opinion, the most striking feature of the building was a tower, covered by a dome of copper and surmounted by a fine vane of beaten copper which represented a ship in sail. In addition, had he been able to see it clearly, he would have noted that the upper part of the tower was decorated with seated figures, sculpted in Portland stone. These figures, according to the details which were given to the press, represented Commerce, Discovery, Shipbuilding and Engineering. There was much to admire inside the building, too, for it was clear from the furnishings and décor that no expense had been spared. Screens and desks in the shipping office were made from polished teak with bronze fittings, the floor was carpeted throughout, and the room was enhanced by a domed roof of 'an artistic design' which contained 'stained-glass medallions with heads typifying the winds of each point of the compass'. However, it was the boardroom which made the biggest impact on visitors that day nearly a century ago. The journalist used 'sumptuous' to describe it, and few would have argued with his choice of word. Here, the room was lined by a teak dado, while the windows were decorated with tinted glass of amorial design. The solid teak board-table was the centre piece of what was a magnificent room, for it was 27 feet 6 inches long by 16 feet 6 inches wide, supported by twenty seven massive turned and moulded panelled legs of original design. The surface of the table was lined with a blue cloth with a moulded teak margin. Around the table stood thirty matching chairs with the backs covered in crimson Morocco leather, each of which carried the Harbour Trust crest as the centre-piece of its design. The chairman's seat had the same crest carved out of its solid oak back. A feature of the whole building was the availability of electric lighting and hot water, the former delivered via 'handsome electrolliers'.

In describing this scene of a century ago, one may be forgiven for conceiving of it as an example of long-gone standards, of a world in which excellence was the expectation of those who were in a position to buy the best. Yet, whilst craftsmen of the old school are few and far between today, the fundamental attitudes which their work embodied are still alive and well, with quality and service being the key elements.

More than fifteen years ago, Tom Peters wrote *In Search of Excellence*. In this and subsequent books, he reminded his readers of the potential impact of the attitudes of managers with regard to the provision of excellent service. Many companies, he noted, espouse a doctrine of superb quality of product and service, but few seem to deliver that promise. Accepting Peters's observation, those who provide the service at Morgans aim to be among the élite in this regard, for it makes good business sense to do so! One thing is certain, in pursuing that goal, staff and management alike will be constantly reminded by the unique building within which they work that business excellence *Is* Achievable, *Is* Rewarding and *Is* Essential for success.

Note

The management would like you to accept this copy of the biography of James Livingston as a souvenir of your visit to Morgans Hotel. The relevance of the subject of the biography to the foregoing will become clear as Livingston's story unfolds. Suffice to say, at this point, that he was a member of the Harbour Trust board for three decades, he was present at the official opening of the new building, he attended the first meeting to be held in it, and was an influential figure in the growth of trade in the port for over forty years. Reading his story will provide you with an insight into the lives of people in Swansea during the fifty years before the Harbour Trust building was opened until the old patriarch died in 1912.

As yet there are no recorded incidents of ghosts stalking the corridors of this house. However, given the rich history of the building, it would be foolish to rule out the possibility.

THE AUTHORS

Dr. DAVID FARMER was born in Manselton and is Professor Emeritus at Henley the Management College, where, until his retirement, he was deputy principal. David was educated at Dynevor School and the universities of Manchester and Bath. A prolific writer in his own field, he is the author or co-author of more than twenty books (one currently in its ninth edition) and more than one hundred papers, articles and business case studies. Since retirement he has turned to local history as a field of interest, and, in the last decade has published several books including a biography of John Humphrey (architect), another of Ivor Allchurch (with Peter Stead), a history of Swansea Rugby Club, a history of Swansea soccer club (with Colin Jones and Brian Lile) and, *Giants of Post-War Welsh Rugby* (with Clive Rowlands), a book which raised £23,000 for the Tŷ Olwen hospice, of which he is deputy chairman.

BRIAN LILE was brought up in Killay, and was educated at Bishop Gore Grammar School, Swansea, and the University of Wales, Aberystwyth. He has also written on Petty Officer Edgar Evans, RN (in *Maritime Wales*), the Williamses of Killay House (*Gower*), the Gower visits of the Reverend Francis Kilvert (*Gower* – with the late Howard Godfrey – and the *Kilvert Society Newsletter*) and, with David Farmer, the early years of association football in south Wales (*Transactions of the Honourable Society of Cymmrodorion*). Now retired, he was formerly on the staff of the National Library of Wales.

THE
REMARKABLE
JAMES LIVINGSTON

DAVID FARMER & BRIAN LILE

Published by
THE ROYAL INSTITUTION OF SOUTH WALES
IN CONJUNCTION WITH MORGANS HOTEL

Copyright © 2002 David Farmer & Brian Lile

Published by
The Royal Institution of South Wales
in conjunction with Morgans Hotel, Swansea.

The right of David Farmer & Brian Lile to be identified as the Authors
of the Work has been asserted by them in accordance with
the Copyright, Designs and Patents Act 1988.

*All rights reserved. No part of this publication may be
reproduced, stored in a retrieval system or transmitted, in any
form or by any means without the prior permission of the
publisher, nor be otherwise circulated in any form of binding
or cover other than that in which it is published and without
similar conditon being imposed on the subsequent purchaser.*

A CIP catalogue record for this book is
available from the British Library.

ISBN 0-9508-5174-4

Cover design:
Ewens Graphic Design
45 Notts Gardens, Uplands, Swansea, SA2 0RU
Telephone: (01792) 201109

Printed in Wales by
Gwasg Dinefwr Press Ltd.,
Rawlings Road, Llandybïe
Carmarthenshire, SA18 3YD
Telephone: (01269) 850576

Contents

List of Illustrations	6
Acknowledgements	7
Foreword by Professor Sir Glanmor Williams	9
Introduction	11
Chapter 1 – Early Interventions	19
Chapter 2 – The Mind	25
Chapter 3 – The Body	33
Chapter 4 – Temperance	44
Chapter 5 – The Wesleyan Connection and Family Life	52
Chapter 6 – The Workingmen's Club and the YMCA	60
Chapter 7 – Swansea Docks and the Chamber of Commerce	70
Chapter 8 – Local Government	81
Chapter 9 – Further Activities	95
Epilogue	104
Bibliography	110
Index	113

Illustrations

Each of the illustrations used in this book is listed below together with a source reference. Reasonable care has been taken to ensure that the proper sources are identified and appropriately acknowledged. We are grateful for the assistance of the organisations listed in allowing us to reproduce these illustrations free of charge.

Page

James Livingston	– Swansea Chamber of Commerce	13
The Reverend Burnard Squire Vicar of Swansea, 1846-76	– Royal Institution of South Wales	22
Wesley Chapel, Goat Street	– Royal Institution of South Wales	27
James Livingston, golfer	– *Cambria Daily Leader*	37
All Whites v. Barbarians – 1905	– N. Starmer-Smith	40
Cycle racing at St. Helen's	– Royal Institution of South Wales	43
Brunswick Chapel	– Swansea Central Reference Library	54
Swansea Workingmen's Club	– Swansea Central Reference Library	61
YMCA appeal	– Swansea Central Reference Library	67
Harbour Trust offices	– Swansea Central Reference Library	73
Loading coal	– Swansea Central Reference Library (Gareth Mills Collection)	75
Swansea Council members	– H. Chapman/*Western Mail*	81
Island House	– Swansea Central Reference Library	88
Cameron Arms	– Swansea Central Reference Library	88
Local election cartoon	– *Cambria Daily Leader*	92

Acknowledgements

Inevitably, a book that has taken many months to research and write will have involved many people other than the authors. Because this is so, it is appropriate for us to thank those who have helped us in any way as we have sought to find out as much as we could about James Livingston. Much information was obtained from the *Cambrian* and the *Cambria Daily Leader,* newspapers which are available at the Swansea Central Reference Library; the National Library of Wales, Aberystwyth, and the Swansea Museum archive. We have used all three facilities in researching this book and we are extremely grateful to the staff at each location, particularly MARILYN JONES and PAT PERKINS at the reference library at Alexandra Road, MICHAEL GIBB and BERNICE CARDY at the museum archive, and GERALD GABB for useful guidance on sources of material. Thanks are due, too to ELIZABETH BENNETT and SUE THOMAS of the University of Wales, Swansea (archive department), and KIM COLLIS at the archive department at County Hall. Once again, we were fortunate to have such ready response to our continuing requests. At the University of Wales, Swansea archive we were given access to the records of the Swansea and Gower Methodist Circuit, which are in their care. The archivist for the Methodist circuit, GREN NEILSON, who directed us to the collection, deserves our sincere thanks in that regard. We were particularly appreciative of Gren's kindness in making available to us the script of a fascinating talk by a former pupil about the period when our subject was Sunday school superintendent at Wesley Chapel in Swansea's Goat Street.

We appreciated the assistance of DR. DAVID JENKINS of the National Museums and Galleries of Wales who was helpful to us with respect to the Cory family, TANIA HEWSON of the YMCA at Swansea for allowing us access to that organisation's Swansea archive, and PHILLIPA BASSETT of the University of Birmingham for providing material from the national YMCA archive. We are grateful to them all, as we are to BERNARD JONES, the secretary of Caradoc Lodge of the Freemasons, for searching for and finding record books and other material relating to the time when

Livingston was Worshipful Master of that organisation. Throughout the writing of this book we have been privileged to be able to call upon the sage advice of PROFESSOR SIR GLANMOR WILLIAMS. As he has on several previous occasions, not only did he offer constructive comments on the work as it developed, he also provided us with motivational asides which were greatly appreciated. We are grateful, too, for his kindness in writing the foreword to this book. We also acknowledge the willing assistance of DAVID PRICE, the archivist for Swansea Cricket and Football Club, for entrusting us with irreplaceable documents, which proved to be very helpful, and LYN HARRIS of Swansea's Chamber of Commerce for her help regarding that institution. HELEN JENKINS, BARBARA PAULDING, and the REVEREND IVOR REES also assisted us and we are grateful. In addition, we express our gratitude to 'ROG', who painted the telling caricature which adorns the cover of this book, and MARTIN EWENS, who converted our rough design into the finished cover. We also greatly appreciated the professionalism of our printers, EMYR, EDDIE and STEPHEN at Dinefwr Press, who provided us with excellent service during the production phase of the book. Finally, we wish to thank the RISW council, our publishers, particularly JENNIFER SABINE, who liaised with us, and BRIAN SIMPSON, who marketed the book, for their willing collaboration in the management of the project. We are grateful, too, to MARTIN and LOUISA MORGAN, of Morgans Hotel for enabling the publication of this book. Without that support the story of the remarkable James Livingston might still be known to very few.

Foreword
by
PROFESSOR SIR GLANMOR WILLIAMS

H. M. Stanley's discovery of David Livingstone in Darkest Africa is one of the most celebrated episodes in nineteenth-century history. The unveiling of the existence of his namesake James Livingston in Victorian Swansea by Professor David Farmer and Mr Brian Lile is, in its own way, nearly as remarkable. James Livingston, so well-known to his contemporaries and so genuinely admired by them, was almost completely forgotten after his death and finds no more than a brief passing mention in only two books on nineteenth-century Swansea. The authors of this admirable volume are sincerely to be commended on rescuing him from undeserved anonymity and for bringing him vividly back to life in this absorbing study of a fascinating individual.

The man here portrayed was, like his more famous namesake, a quintessential Victorian. True to the age in which he lived, his character was rooted in his unshakeable religious convictions. His driving sense of duty, service, purpose, industry and incessant labour, all sprang from an undeviating commitment to his Christian faith. Born of Scottish ancestry in Boulston, Pembrokeshire, in 1831, partly educated in France, he came to Swansea in the early 1850s, set up successfully in business, and spent the rest of his days there until his death in 1912. He became a prosperous business man and a prominent figure in religious, commercial, sporting, political and local government circles, throwing himself with boundless zest and vigour into an extraordinarily wide spectrum of interests. A man of powerful frame, commanding presence and inexhaustible energy, he was a most eloquent speaker and fiery debater, and a gifted, far-seeing administrator, although not blessed with the gift of easily tolerating dissent or suffering fools gladly. He, in fact, confessed himself to be 'a stubborn, independent, pig-headed man'.

Whatever may have been his shortcomings, he bestowed a wealth of gifts upon the whole range of Swansea's institutions: its docks, shipping, trade, railways, roads, tramways, local government and politics, and its accounts and finances. He was a leading light in its education, chapels, Sunday schools, temperance causes, Workingmen's Club, YMCA, Freemasons, rugby, cricket and athletic clubs. When he died in 1912, a press obituary justly concluded, 'Swansea has, unquestionably lost one of its foremost citizens, a man of sterling ability, and above all, a man of character . . . leaving a void that may not for many years, if ever, be filled' (*Cambria Daily Leader*). The writer expressed no more than the simple truth. What neither he nor anyone else foresaw was that James Livingston's name would pass into unmerited oblivion. He was worthy of much more honourable recognition, and has at last received it. He now takes his rightful place alongside the giants of Victorian Swansea, men like Lewis Weston Dillwyn, Sir John Llewelyn, or William Thomas of Lan. Professor Farmer and Mr Lile deserve our most cordial congratulations for having so carefully researched and attractively written such a lifelike portrait of a truly outstanding, if hitherto strangely ignored, Swansea figure.

Professor Sir Glanmor Williams

On his retirement from the Chair of History at the University of Wales, Swansea, a volume of essays was presented to Professor Sir Glanmor Williams. It was a compilation of the writings of 'thirteen scholars, several of whom were among Britain's foremost historians' and its fly leaf referred to him as 'the most distinguished Welsh historian of his generation'. It would be difficult to find anyone with an interest in Welsh history to disagree with that description.

What is, perhaps, less well-known about Sir Glanmor is the guidance and encouragement which he has given to hundreds of people who have set out to make some contribution to Welsh history. This book is, certainly, the better for his sage advice.

Introduction

An intriguing problem which faces anyone undertaking historical research can best be described by using the analogy of a street map. The researcher's planned route may be thought of as proceeding along Main Street, but en route he or she finds that several tempting side streets present themselves for investigation. In most cases, given that there is some deadline by when the planned work has to be completed, the focused researcher has little option other than to avoid these diversions. Nevertheless, there are instances when a particular name or topic is referred to on several occasions, which reinforces the attraction of that particular side street. In such cases the preliminary outlines of another project may emerge, leading the researcher concerned to return in order to convert the interesting byways into a new Main Street. So it was with the subject of this book.

The name James Livingston first came to the attention of one of the present authors whilst researching the history of Swansea Rugby Club.[1] Livingston became closely involved with that organisation and with several other sporting activities in the town. He was chairman of Swansea Cricket and Football Club, he became vice-president of the Swansea Rugby Club and was concerned with the founding of the Welsh Rugby Union (of which he became vice-president). But that was not all; he was involved with athletics, road walking, sea-rowing and other healthy activities, and held office in a number of the organisations in these fields of activity. When the Swansea Workingmen's Club was established he became president or chairman of a number of its sections, and in conjunction with Sir John Llewelyn and William Thomas of Lan, he was instrumental in saving St. Helen's field from the developers of his day. His influence on the development of the port and town of Swansea through his business, his work for the Chamber of Commerce, and in local government was marked by a number of major successes, and there were many other positive outcomes to projects with which he was involved. At the heart of all this work was his unswerving dedication to the task of trying to live a Christian life. Some of those who opposed him on certain issues might have argued about his interpretation of what this meant, but the scope and quality of his selfless dedication to serving his fellow man spoke volumes for his sincerity.

Subsequent research showed that this impressive list of James Livingston's activities represented only part of the remarkable range of his creative and effective interventions in the life of Victorian and Edwardian Swansea. It was little wonder then that in the report of his death in the *Cambria Daily Leader* of 9 January 1912, the writer should eulogise:

> Swansea, by the passing of Cllr. James Livingston, JP, has unquestionably lost one of its finest citizens; a man of sterling ability, a man capable of inspiring public affairs; above and beyond all, a man of character. To say that he will be missed is not enough; the fact is that Mr Livingston leaves a void that may not for years, if ever, be filled in the corporate and social life of Swansea.

As the authors discovered when undertaking the research for this publication, and as the reader will perceive from the story as it unfolds, the tone and content of the *Leader* eulogy would appear to be thoroughly justified. Consequently, the fact that it has taken a century since his death for the story of this outstanding citizen to be told, is itself something of an enigma. It is also puzzling that in the growing body of literature concerned with the history of Swansea, James Livingston is rarely mentioned. For example, Livingston was a coal exporter of some substance and considerable longevity. He was twice president of the Chamber of Commerce, he was the town's mayor, and was a member of the Harbour Trust committee. Consequently, it would be reasonable to expect that W. H. Jones in his landmark *History of the Port of Swansea,* would have mentioned Livingston's contribution to several of the major projects associated with the development of the port which were extensively reported in the contemporary press. Instead, his name appears just once, and that in a footnote. Jones writes: 'As a harbour trustee, he [Frank Ash Yeo, MP, JP] with Mr James Livingston, specially exerted himself to secure the deepening of the harbour in preparation for the great development of steam power which was then advancing.'[2]

Brief though it is, this is at least one indication of Livingston's efforts to further the interests of the town and port in which he lived; only one of the other publications concerned with Swansea's history makes any reference

INTRODUCTION

James Livingston at the beginning of his second term as president of Swansea Chamber of Commerce (1905).

at all to that work. Yet, having spent many hours researching the man's life, the authors are convinced that Livingston was more than worthy of frequent mention. To put that claim into perspective, it is interesting to consider Professor Sir Glanmor Williams's introduction to the facsimile edition of W. H. Jones's work. Sir Glanmor, in referring to the author, notes that 'he was not chary of criticizing the initial dilatoriness, approaching indolence of the earliest trustees.' But he had 'nothing save praise for those men of unbounded energy who were later not only to urge forward the improvement of harbour facilities but also see them executed'.[3] By implication, at least, W. H. Jones's footnote includes Livingston among those men of unbounded energy. The present authors believe that the reader will come to the same conclusion, as have they; for there is no doubt that he deserves such recognition. Perhaps, local historians of the past may not have been lured, as we were, by the attractions of byways from which the name and activities of James Livingston shone with such an appealing glow. Certainly, in researching and writing this book, the authors have been privileged and inspired by the subject's talents, energy, character, vision and determination, whilst accepting his sometimes idiosyncratic approach to his life of service as an intriguing element of his personality. We trust that what we have written will do justice to the life of this truly remarkable man and ensure his place in the annals of Swansea, port and town.

Livingston's Environment

To place the story of Livingston's life in context, it is important to acknowledge the impact which contemporary attitudes and influences have on individuals and society at a particular time in history. Asa Briggs tells us something of those which characterized the Victorian era and which, as he puts it, 'conditioned the national mood' during that period in Britain's history.[4] Then Britain was prosperous, it was the world's workshop, the world's shipbuilder, carrier, clearing house and banker. There was a warm sense of national security in the country, for 'Britain ruled the waves' and because that was so, neither the supremacy nor the independence of the nation was ever threatened. The country's major institutions were seen as being inviolable – the old saying 'safe as the Bank of England' being indicative of this. Underpinning all these things were a widely held belief in a common moral code based on duty and self-restraint, and a new emphasis on education for the masses as well as the privileged few. In turn, self-education and self-help (à la Samuel Smiles) were promoted extensively.

All these things touched Swansea. It was a prosperous place, and, like many other towns in Britain, was one in which class differences, particularly in terms of working and living conditions, were etched into the fabric of society. It was a place, too, where the teachings of the chapels and churches of the day influenced the common moral code. Taken as a whole, it was an environment within which effective reforming zeal had scope to flourish, if only in terms of improving the lot of the working man. In Swansea, the evidence of such zeal is perpetuated, for example, by the statue in the city's Victoria Park of the 'champion of open spaces', William Thomas of Lan.[5] Thomas, it was, who persuaded John Dillwyn Llewelyn to donate part of his estate to the people of Swansea and who, together with the latter's son, John and the subject of this book, fought elements within the council and the developers to preserve St. Helen's field for the same purpose.

Swansea at the time was a fast developing town; a place where a young man with vision and entrepreneurial skills could make his way. James Livingston was such a man, though his objectives for personal advancement were heavily influenced by a desire to help improve the lot of his fellow man. This embraced, for example, the promotion and development of more effective government of the town of Swansea, and its greater competitiveness as a commercial seaport; the promotion of healthy outdoor activities for the masses; involvement in the provision of facilities to help develop the minds of the labouring classes, and in the movement to minimize the detrimental effects of the use and abuse of alcohol. All of which is indicative of the scope of Livingston's contribution to Swansea. The *Leader* tribute had it that he was 'a man of character'. That, plus seemingly unbounded energy, coupled with a fine stature and outstanding communication skills, helped set James Livingston aside in the annals of the town of Swansea, although, as has been stated, it has taken some time for his contribution to Swansea, town and port to be acknowledged.

We have to confess at the outset that It has not been possible to ascertain certain details concerning Livingston's background and that, despite our best efforts, we are left with a number of unanswered questions. We know from census returns and parish registers that he was born at 'Shady Grove', East Wood in the Pembrokeshire parish of Boulston, some three miles south of Haverfordwest in August 1831. He was one of at least seven children of William Livingston, agricultural labourer, and his wife Mary, née Phillips. William, of Scottish descent, was born at Roch, near Newgale, while his wife hailed from Wiston, near Haverfordwest. We have established that their son, James received part of his education as a pupil at the École des Anglais in Paris and that he was there at the same time as one Thomas Cory. However, it remains a mystery as to how he came to have the privilege of such an education when his father had such a humble occupation. It is tempting to suggest a situation in which some benefactor identified the lad's potential early in his life and, as a result, sponsored his education. If that is true, who was this person? Was he, for example Thomas Cory's father, or was he some grandee of Pembrokeshire society? Judging by James Livingston's life and career, whoever he was, it is fair to say that his perception of the boy's potential was admirable. Apart from Livingston's entrepreneurial and management abilities as a trader, many of his interventions in the administration of the affairs of his adopted town were notable for their success. He also developed wide-ranging social skill, which enabled him to relate to the working man as readily as he did to the captains of commerce, or the members of the great Swansea families of his era.

The fact that he was held in great esteem by many in all strata of local society suggests that Livingston was an urbane, even if sometimes dour man. Certainly, as we shall see in the chapters which follow, there were occasions when he dug in his heels and would not be persuaded to concede his position. Our conclusion is that he was not only a man of character he was also, a man whose standards and principles were of the highest order. Furthermore, throughout his life in Swansea, he endeavored to practise what he preached. His was a life of service to his community and to his God, and like John Wesley – the founder of Methodism, the branch of nonconformity which Livingston heartily embraced – he served on almost to the end of his life. Indeed, days before he died, he was re-elected (without opposition) to the borough council as the councillor for Victoria Ward and was reappointed as chairman of the Joint Asylum Committee (Merthyr and Swansea) which was one of the projects which he had championed during his life in Swansea. Since he was eighty-one at the time, these appointments are indicative of not only the longevity of the service he rendered but also to the quality of his work.

In closing this brief introduction, it is interesting to note that Livingston took his Christian principles into all aspects of his life. To use a modern term, there was a seamless continuum between Livingston's church, business, community and social activities. No suit for Sunday and another for the remaining six days for him. No doubt, his detractors might have interpreted things differently, but he faced the challenges of his life confident in his interpretation of what was expected of him as a believing Christian. Having spent many hours learning about James Livingston and knowing that he was a local preacher for almost a half century, we are aware that, in the course of that time, he would have preached sermons based upon several hundred biblical texts. What they were we shall never know, but were we asked to select two verses which appear to fit our subject and reflect the ethos of his life we would cite: 'However, by God's grace I am what I am, nor has his grace been given to me in vain; on the contrary, in my labours I have outdone them all – not I, indeed, but the grace of God working with me',[6] and, 'Does this sound as if I am trying to gain man's approval? No indeed. What I want is God's approval! Am I trying to be popular with men? If I were still trying to do I could not be a servant of Christ.'[7]

Giving service to his fellow man was at the heart of the many Livingston ventures which are described in this book. He believed that God was working through him and gave his all in many causes. His interventions in seeking to improve the lot of the working man provide just one example and he did this work without self-interest. Furthermore, it will be clear to the reader that he undertook these tasks without concern for personal popularity. It is probable that he believed that enhancing the condition of the mind, body and spirit of an individual could lead to the sum of the whole being greater than the sum of the parts, hence his intrusion into healthy sport, church life, temperance, and the development of the mind. His Chamber of Commerce and local government activities typically focussed on improving the quality and range of services and, idiosyncratic though he was at times, he continued working in this way virtually until his death in 1912.

Coupled with his Christian faith, the Latin tag *Mens sana in corporo sano* (A healthy mind in a healthy body) appears to have been at the heart of James Livingston's philosophy of life. This became increasingly clear to us during the research phase of this book as we learned more about this remarkable man, for it was reflected in the way he lived and the focus of what he tried to do to help others. By adding spirit to 'mind' and 'body', he sought to influence the whole person. The structure of this book is based upon that thinking. While most of the chapters are written with a focus upon one element of the whole, or one segment of Livingston's life, the common theme is evident. As will be seen from the illustrations that are used throughout the book, the elements are not mutually exclusive. For example, 'education' is a many faceted topic, and Livingston worked hard and long to influence the minds of young people and old through temperance work, Sunday school teaching, preaching, debating and lecturing, and in developing subordinates in business and in other organisations. Chapter 1 is intended, as it were, as a preliminary sketch to give the reader an early insight into the character of James Livingston. Chapters 2, 3, 4 and 5 each focus upon one of the elements of what we believe was his philosophy of life. Chapters 6, 7 and 8 are each concerned with one of the major activities of Livingston's life. Chapter 9 is intended to embrace other fields of activity; the epilogue is to draw the book to a conclusion.

REFERENCES

1. David Farmer, *The All Whites*, Swansea: DFPS. 1995.
2. W. H. Jones, *History of the Port of Swansea*, Carmarthen: Spurrell, 1922; Facsim. ed. [Swansea], West Glamorgan Archive Service, 1995, p. 214.
3. Glanmor Williams, in Jones, op. cit.
4. Asa Briggs, *Victorian People: A Reassessment of Persons and Themes, 1851-1867*. London: Oldhams, 1954; Folio Society, 1996, pp. 2, 3, 4.
5. See: J. Alun Owen, *Swansea's Earliest Open Spaces: A Study of Swansea's Parks and Their Promoters in the Nineteenth Century*. Swansea: Swansea City Council, 1995, pp. 43-8.
6. Holy Bible. 1 Corinthians 15:10.
7. Galatians 1:10.

CHAPTER 1

Early Interventions

It is probable that James Livingston first came to Swansea to live and work during 1855 following the completion of his education in Paris. An intelligent and personable young man, either through his own initiative or as a result of an introduction from his benefactor, or both, he would not have found it difficult to find an opening in one of the many trading businesses which flourished in Swansea at that time. Everything else apart, he was fluent in French, a considerable advantage when that language was used worldwide in commercial transactions. We know that, on arrival in the town, he attended the Wesleyan Methodist Chapel in Goat Street, that he lived at the time in Cradock Street and was married at Wesley in April 1859. His bride, who had been a resident at Cleveland Terrace and was fellow member of that chapel, Mary Jane Brewer, was two years his junior and the daughter of a master mariner. Presumably, Livingston's new father-in-law had satisfied himself as to the young man's career prospects before giving his blessing to the union. If so, the sailor's judgement would have been sound, for, in its edition for 1866/7, *Slater's Directory of Swansea*[1] lists the firm Richards and Livingston, Shipbrokers and Merchants of 1 Mount Street, as agents for Nantmelin Colliery, Merthyr, in the export of steam coal. He had established himself, at the age of 35, as a member of Swansea's commercial élite. He was established, too, as the head of a family: by then, Mary Jane had borne him two daughters and a son.

It was in the following year that Livingston made one of his early forays into civic matters in Swansea. In June 1866, at a meeting of the Corporation and Local Board of Health, there was an earnest discussion regarding the serious outbreak of yellow fever which had occurred in the port during the previous September.[2] In order to ensure that the town might be better prepared to deal with such matters, the authorities had decided to utilise Burrows Lodge, a large house situated where today's Leisure Centre stands, as a fever and cholera hospital. Clearly, Livingston had been involved in a movement to overturn this decision, for, after the presentation of a strongly worded petition from 'inhabitants and ratepayers of the town and borough', he rose to second the proposal of the petitioners. He argued that the choice of Burrows Lodge was the worst possible one, because it was contiguous to the South Dock and the principal thoroughfares of the town. He stressed that the site of the building, were it used for the purposes suggested would have 'a prejudicial effect upon trade and commerce, and upon its shipping . . . on which the town mainly depends'. He went on to argue that the statistics which the petitioners gathered prove that the yellow fever epidemic had reduced exports by half. In his opinion, if the site for the hospital was approved, within one month our dock would be emptied and commerce gone. Livingston's was a formidable presentation, which brought the young man to the attention of the leading figures of the town. Among those who supported him was John Llewelyn and, judging by subsequent developments, it is clear that the Tory landowner was impressed by what he heard and saw of the independent, liberally minded young businessman. Llewelyn must have been impressed, too, by the force of the overall argument from the petitioners, for the Burrows Lodge decision was overturned.

From James Livingston's own point of view, it is tempting to suggest that his involvement in managing and presenting the petition had an impact upon his own thinking and motivation concerning his rôle in the life of the town of Swansea. Perhaps it illustrated for him the style of intervention which would be beneficial for the greater good of the town's people, and may have given him the confidence to apply his mind and energies to such activity. On the other hand, it could be argued that by involving himself in the yellow fever petition he was simply looking after his own interests. The fact that he had such interests cannot be denied. However, given the scope and focus of his many interventions during his long life, it would be extremely difficult to sustain the argument that self-interest was all that really counted with him.

The Church Rates Controversy

Two years after the yellow fever epidemic had been dealt with, the name of James Livingston was to the fore again in the town of Swansea. This time he was to make a personal stand on a controversial issue over which he confronted the Establishment in the interests of what he believed to be for the greater good. In so doing he caused distress to his own wife, who was far from well, while he underwent a legal process which could have resulted in a social stigma being attached to his person. In due course, those who brought the action argued that Livingston must have been aware of the consequences of his stand, which, in all probability, was true. Nevertheless, that did not deter him.

In 1867, the year when Livingston made his stand, and for many years before, the Church of England expected the people who lived in any parish under its jurisdiction to pay tithes to their local vicar. These taxes were intended to allow for the maintenance of the fabric of parish church buildings. Not surprisingly, given the number of nonconformist churches which had been and were being built, there were many thousands of Dissenters who were unhappy with this requirement. Why, these people asked, should we pay for something, which we do not use? They paid, they said, to maintain their own chapels and did not ask anything of the Established Church.

These were reasonable arguments, which had been in vogue up and down the country since the successful action in 1841 at Rochdale by the reformer, John Bright.[3] Bright's Lancashire success, however, was not repeated in many other places, although Dissenters in various towns continued to campaign for the law to be changed. For example, in south Wales, the Reverend David Rees, the minister of Capel Als in Llanelli, led an ongoing campaign for many years which highlighted the inequalities of the tithe system. Rees, an articulate and intelligent man, used every channel of communication at his disposal to present his arguments. He carried on his crusade largely in the Welsh language, but it is likely that Livingston, although not a Welsh speaker, would have known of the minister's activities. In making his case, however, the Swansea man focused upon a particular issue, which other reformers had not highlighted. After the event, well aware of the benefits of using the media, he presented his arguments in a letter to the *Cambrian*.

Under the heading, 'The vicar of St. Mary's and his tithes', he wrote:

> I have just had my furniture seized by the Rev. E. B. Squires for tithes . . . said to be payable on the field on part of which my home stands. I suppose that a small amount is due, which, if he as vicar

*The Reverend Burnard Squire,
Vicar of Swansea, 1846-76.*

had asked me I would have paid. But what right has Mr Squire or anybody else, to call upon me to pay the total amount due on twenty or thirty homes? This is what he asked me to do, and, because I refused, he, in my absence sent four bailiffs, headed by an auctioneer and accompanied by a town crier, to take possession of my furniture. My wife who is in a delicate state of health, was very much terrified . . . and all this to fill Mr Squire's purse.

From this distance, it would appear that Livingston's objection to having to act as a tithe collector for the vicar is perfectly understandable. Yet the practice was commonplace throughout the land. Livingston, whilst decrying this process also had another complaint about its application. The normal procedure involved the Church authorities in selecting one householder to collect the money due from the houses in that district. Livingston noted that 'year after year he [the vicar] selects people whom he probably knows to be Dissenters to carry out the task on his behalf. Why does he not fix upon some person who does him the honour of attending his church?'

In subsequent editions of the *Cambrian* several letters were published which supported one side or the other. In the main, those which took the side of the Established Church argued for the *status quo* and for obeying the law of the land; and, in one case, the writer made an appeal 'to our common Christianity'. Finally, it was Livingston who brought the correspondence to a close through a long letter in which he reiterated his key arguments and responded to those which his opponents had raised. He began: 'This letter is far too long, but really I have no time to curtail it' and concluded: 'In calling the attention of my neighbours to the matter of tithes and the way they are collected, I feel satisfied that I have only done what was right . . . so I leave it to the public.' James Livingston was, of course, referring to the people of Swansea, but within twelve months the representatives of a far wider public voted on the matter, when the Tithe Rent Charge Act, 1891 was passed at Westminster. Whilst Livingston was delighted with this news, his pleasure was marred by the death of his wife soon after the change in law was announced. He must have agonised as to whether her death had been hastened by the incident with the bailiffs. We shall never know, but, since he was to make many further personal stands in his lifetime, it seems likely that he accepted her death as the will of God.

In concluding this chapter it is interesting to note that among the letters from Establishment correspondents concerning the matter, was one from an E. G. Williams in which the writer described his first meeting with Livingston: 'When he joined others on the platform . . . on the occasion of some agitation against the powers that be . . . judging from what I saw and heard it did not seem to indicate a feeling of small beer'. From this it would appear that the writer was attempting to label Livingston as an agitator who liked the sound of his own voice. There is no doubt that he did campaign, time and again, against the *status quo*, although only for causes in which he believed, which, usually, proved to be concerned with the common good. As for his speaking style, in the *Cambria Daily Leader* notice of his death, the writer stated that Livingston had 'a capital platform manner'. The paper might have added that it was a talent, which he used to the advantage of many causes, which he supported throughout his life. Indeed, it is the contention of the authors that, given his staunch beliefs and his many forays, which were intended to improve the lot of his fellow man, personal ego appears to have played a minor part in the process.

REFERENCES

1. *Slater's Directory of Swansea*. London: Isaac Slater, 1866/7.
2. P. D. Meers, 'Yellow fever in Swansea, 1865', *The Journal of Hygiene*, 97 (1986), pp. 185-91. On 9 September 1865, during a period of exceptionally hot weather, the barque *Hecla*, carrying copper ore from Cuba, tied up in Swansea's North Dock. At nine that morning a sick member of the crew was carried ashore and taken to a local lodging house, where, at midday, he died of yellow fever. Thirteen days later a resident of the town succumbed to the same disease. The Registrar of Births and Deaths notified the Registrar General in London and a Dr. George Buchanan was sent to Swansea to conduct an investigation. During the next twenty-five days at least twenty-seven inhabitants were recorded as being infected with the disease, of whom fifteen died. The outbreak still remains as the largest yellow fever epidemic recorded in the UK.
3. Asa Briggs, op. cit., pp. 172-3.

CHAPTER 2

The Mind

As is indicated in the introduction to this book, the environment in which James Livingston lived and worked, was conducive to his cause. Self-help, self-education through workingmen's clubs, a common moral code which was shaped by the teachings of the chapels and churches in the area, were among the helpful factors in the environment. There was also a well-established concern for the secular education of children in the church which he attended. The leaders of the Wesleyan Chapel in Goat Street had established a day school in 1805 and at the time of Livingston's arrival in Swansea, it was providing a basic general education, underpinned by Christian values, for 180 pupils. In the years before educational emancipation, this service met a vital need in a community where life was hard and the majority of workers were uneducated. Consequently, Livingston had significant support for his initiatives from like-minded people in his church community and elsewhere in Swansea. In retrospect, he can be seen to have been the right man in the right place at the right time. Nevertheless, any person wishing to achieve a set of objectives, to employ a sailing analogy, has to use the prevailing wind to best advantage. James Livingston did that. In the process he gained a reputation as an influential leader and educator of young people.

Initially, outside his challenging full-time occupation, and his church and temperance work, Livingston concentrated his weekday efforts on the education and development of working men who had not been fortunate enough to receive even a rudimentary education. Not that he ignored the educational needs of children. As will be seen later in this chapter, he was most concerned about such issues. In the field of adult education, he used a variety of means to help satisfy these needs. For example, he was associated with Swansea Young Men's Christian Association (YMCA) from its earliest days, being appointed the branch's first president in 1867, and was involved in the management of Swansea Workingmen's Club, being vice-president for several years. In each case he encouraged the establishment of a library, the use of lectures, discussions and debates and, sometimes, straightforward teaching of what were commonly referred to at that time as the 'Three Rs'. A night school approach was used in many cases, and in each organisation he found willing and able people who filled the teacher/tutor roles.

In the present context this provides another insight into the man's approach. In a number of cases he was involved in what management academics today call 'start-up', and then moved on to other work. It was not that he lost interest in a particular venture after it had been established, rather that, given the many organisations with which he was involved, if he was to be successful with his panoramic approach to influencing society, effective delegation was essential. Fortunately, there were many people with the right qualifications in Swansea at the time who could fill such roles more than adequately, allowing Livingston the opportunity to address the broader canvas, or to focus in greater detail where he felt that his own individual set of talents were needed. Over time, especially in his later years, his management of this approach attracted criticism from some quarters, but, as the reader will perceive from the discussion in this book, it seems at this distance to have been a sensible way for the man to deploy his talents and predilections. It is a wise man who understands his strengths and weaknesses and approaches his tasks by taking advantage of those virtues, while recruiting others with different but complementary talents to work with him in order to achieve a particular set of objectives.

In December 1871 the *Aberystwyth Observer* published a report which provides us with further insight into the mind of James Livingston, *vis-à-vis* education. The paper had sent a journalist to cover a meeting of Welsh Liberals which was being held in the town. In a long report of the conference, the newspaperman noted that Livingston had seconded the motion that 'this conference desires the establishment of a truly national system of education, and is of the opinion that the act as prescribed contains provisions that render it impracticable'.[1] Livingston told the delegates that he spoke as a Wesleyan, not as a representative of that body, but as one anxious that his denomination should make a stand on this important question. He went on to argue, with less than delicate frankness, that the most serious aspect was that the Church of England and the Church of Rome had coalesced in order to obtain endowments for their schools out of the rates, a statement which brought a great cheer from the

The Wesleyan Chapel, Goat Street, which Livingston joined on coming to Swansea in 1855.

conference members. He thought that this was a great pity and that nothing would meet the needs of the country 'but a purely secular system of education (cheers)'. Established Church and Catholic members in the hall would not have been among those cheering. However, as a whole, the (presumably predominantly nonconformist) delegates to the conference left no one in doubt that they supported the proposition. Apart from the funding issue, Livingston was also concerned that the education provided by the Church schools would tend to channel the minds of the pupils involved into Anglican or Roman ways. It was a theme to which he would return on many occasions.

Twenty years later, for example, he wrote a letter to the *Cambrian* complaining about a Church of England booklet published for the use of children under the title *No. 1 Confession*. The publication, he noted, had been edited by a 'committee of clergy for the use of children and young people'. He did not mince his words; 'I consider it to be a blasphemous and obscene condition of salvation that our own sons and daughters go on their knees before a priest (a clergyman of the Protestant Church of England) or endure the suffering of the terrible fires of hell.' No doubt, High Church clerics would have viewed such remarks as being the outpourings of an ill-informed Dissenter, but Livingston, believed strongly in the validity of his own position. In keeping with many nonconformists he would have clung to the powerful promise of Jesus Christ that 'where two or three are gathered together in my name there am I in the midst of them'.[2] Priests, he would have argued, are not mentioned in that promise; therefore, there is no need for an intermediary in prayer or in confession. Had there been a debate on the subject, Livingston and a priest of either the Anglican or Roman church would probably have had to agree to differ. What dangers there were, they each may have thought, if the other party had educational jurisdiction over young minds.

Ostensibly, Livingston was arguing for secular education for all, without denominational bias, but he did not help his cause by writing his letter in such stringent language. He could have made his fundamental point more effectively in more considered sentences, but he appears, rather like Tam O'Shanter's wife, to have been nursing his wrath to keep it warm. It is likely that, in one of his classes he would have advised his listeners to keep calm and avoid such emotional outbursts when debating, but then, Livingston, particularly later in his life, would on occasions fail to heed such sound advice. As he himself put it, 'I have never shirked a confrontation yet and I never will'. Like many strong-minded people, his obduracy sometimes came to the fore when his ire was roused. That was rarely to his own advantage or that of the cause which he was supporting. Nevertheless, it is important to recognise that his many successes outnumbered his failures by a significant degree.

Early in his life James Livingston had been fascinated by people who had the ability to speak and debate in public. He was an admirer of the leading preachers of his day and of the most able politicians. He worked hard to develop his own ability as a speaker by watching and listening and, if we are to judge by his eulogy in the *Cambrian*, he was successful, for the paper recorded that he had a 'capital platform manner'. Like many contemporary orators, he sought to dominate his audience and sweep them along with him as he made his points. A big man with a powerful voice, he developed a style of addressing an audience which today would be considered 'over-the-top', but which was typical of the best speakers of the time.[3] Livingston believed that such talent could be developed in people who had the necessary latent abilities. He thought that debating, with its requirement for sound planning, its need for presenting a case convincingly and the ability to analyse information quickly and efficiently while listening to the opponent's arguments, would give the individual considerable confidence when engaged in public speaking. Obviously, these tasks led to the development of the mind and to the acquisition of relevant techniques which would be beneficial in many aspects of life. Because of this, Livingston and others were actively involved in promoting and supporting debating societies in Swansea. By 1862 there were several societies in being in the district. Among them were the Swansea Debating and Literary Society; the Swansea Debating Society, and the Sketty Debating and Drama Society. Other societies with an interest in debate were active at the same time in the town's churches and chapels, in the YMCA and in the Workingmen's Club. If we are to judge by the meetings which were reported in the press, the bigger societies, in particular, encouraged debate on a wide range of topics in the late seventies and early eighties. For example, among the issues debated were: 'The present condition of Ireland is due to the long years of misrule to which that country has been subjected to by the Government of England', and 'This house believes that the Church of England should be disestablished and disendowed'. Clearly, these societies were not afraid to debate contentious matters.

During the next decade, Livingston supported the Mutual Improvement class at York Street Baptist Chapel as well as that at the St. Helen's Workingmen's Institute, which met at the Vincent Street schoolroom. In reporting on an evening at the latter venue, the *Cambrian* stated that 'Mr Livingston addressed the meeting and, with his very eloquent delivery riveted the attention of his audience during a short but telling speech'. Typically, in pressing home his message about the working man taking advantage of such facilities, he thanked the Richardson family for their generosity in providing them.[4]

By the middle of 1881, however, Livingston and his colleagues, being concerned about the level of activity in the various debating societies in the town, called a meeting at the YMCA rooms to consider the matter. According to the *Cambrian*, the convenors of the meeting believed that the intellectual life of the town could be gauged by the success or failure of societies established for the purpose of promoting public discussion. If the paper was right, then, during the previous two decades, the quality of that intellectual activity had fluctuated. At the meeting, Livingston pointed out that there had been periods during these twenty years when young men 'bursting with the desire of eloquent utterance', did not have a place of resort where they might 'display their powers of speech and sharpen their wits by contact with those of other fellows'. It seemed that some of the debating societies which had come into being 'dwindled and died away'. As a consequence, there was a widely held view that the three most active societies should amalgamate in order to ensure that there was a strong debating association worthy of the town. The meeting chaired by Livingston, concurred, and Frank Ash Yeo was elected president, while the chairman of the evening and two others became vice-presidents.

With young men (young ladies, it would appear, were not considered) who wanted to improve their debating abilities being now catered for through the amalgamated society, Livingston moved on. His sound advice to would-be speakers to 'watch, listen and learn from the performances of the outstanding orators of the day' was well-received and, given that there were many 'stars of the pulpit' in Swansea at the time, there were frequent opportunities to do so. Livingston, meantime, no doubt honing his speaking technique by taking his own advice, used them to good effect in his many fields of activity. One metier, which he enjoyed greatly, was lecturing. In particular he and the many gatherings which he addressed enjoyed talks about his travels. The majority of people had never been abroad, thus his description of visits to many parts of Europe attracted large audiences. It has to be said that, whilst these talks were always educational, the informed cynics in his audiences might have bridled at his tendency to exaggerate to make some points. For example, at one meeting in 1888 he lectured on 'Europe, its cities, catacombs, ruins and prisons', a topic which, in the opinion of the *Cambrian*, would 'be sure to afford a pleasant evening's recreation for the mind'. Clearly, he was unimpressed by Madrid, Milan and other European cities; he thought that Swansea Bay was far superior to that of Naples and reported that whilst he was in Naples, Vesuvius had erupted, giving off smoke 'equal to all the chimney stacks of Landore'. With sweeping generalisation he dismissed the French, Italians and Spanish as inferior to the 'Englishman' (there was not much sense of a Welsh identity in those days), while English women were also far superior to their continental sisters. His *pièce de résistance* of hyperbole, however, was a passing comment on Monte Carlo with its 'gambling dens'. It seemed that this nefarious activity resulted in 'three suicides a day'. In a debating situation, an opponent could have had a field day with some of Livingston's comments that evening. Yet it is essential to keep in mind the historical context in which he was speaking. Many Victorian orators, particularly those who sought to entertain, were prone to exaggerate to make a point. Their language and the examples used to illustrate some aspect of argument would frequently lead them to hyperbole – the ends in such cases seemingly justifying the means.

Another of Livingston's lecture topics illustrates other aspects of his work in this field. Having set up the new Swansea Debating and Literary Society with Frank Ash Yeo, he agreed to lecture to the members at an early meeting. The contemporary description of the audience as a 'grand turn-out' suggests something of the quality of his standing. He took as his topic 'The coming federation of English-speaking people in the world' and, after 'persuasive argument' in which he said that he was confident that it would come about, ended his talk with the assertion that it would be productive of universal good. Whether that has been true may be a matter of contention. However, two world wars and almost a century later, a confederation of English-speaking people is a reality. English (or perhaps American), is the common business language at least, and Livingston was thus correct in making the forecast implicit in his title.

Advancing age did little to dim James Livingston's concerns regarding the education of children. At the age of 76, having returned to local politics, he became involved in a conflict between Swansea Council and the managers of Oxford Street Church School. His position remained unchanged. He had advocated the establishment of secular schools without religious teaching, arguing that instructing young people about the Bible and its meaning for them, was a task for the churches and chapels. In the case of Oxford Street School, he contended that he and the council committee which was dealing with the matter, were merely standing for principle. According to Livingston, the Education Act of 1902 had been 'fraudulently obtained in the interests of bishops and High Church men.' He would never pay for religious teaching to which he objected. That, he went on to say was the principle on which they were fighting. Then, he urged the Oxford Street committee and staff to 'protest against your bishops and get them to come to terms with this infamous act on the statute book.'⁵

Three years earlier, he had made his position clear on the matter by citing two principles: taxation and representation must be inseparable, and a creed test must not be used in the selection of teachers in schools supported out of the rates. He argued that the first of these was 'a great constitutional principle', while the latter, if ignored, would inevitably create and perpetuate religious strife. Reading between the lines, it is not difficult to note the situation he favoured. He believed that a teacher who was not a member of the Church of England should have the same opportunity as any member of the Established Church of gaining an appointment at any school which was supported by the rates. As for subsidising church schools out of the rates, that was both unfair and undesirable. Whether the managers of Oxford Street School had any influence on their bishops was also extremely doubtful, and despite Livingston's efforts, in the shorter term, little was to change.

REFERENCES

1. The Education Act (1871).
2. Holy Bible, Matthew 18:20.
3. See, for example, Kenneth O. Morgan, *Rebirth of a Nation: Wales, 1880-1980*. London: Oxford University Press, 1982, p. 18. 'Ultimately, one suspects, the "big guns" of the pulpit gained their mass appeal not from the theoretical or the literary content of their fiery sermons but from the populist impact of their own personalities'.
4. John Richardson came to Swansea in 1825 and founded a shipping/trading dynasty which became one of the most powerful in the town. In particular, the family prospered at the height of the copper smelting boom. They supported numerous causes in Swansea, among them the St. Helen's Workingmen's Institute. See: R. J. Hart, 'The Richardsons', *Minerva*, Vol. IX (2001).
5. The Education Act (1902). As Morgan (op. cit., pp. 37-8) points out, Lloyd George was closely involved in the Welsh 'revolt' against this act.

CHAPTER 3

The Body

Very little information exists regarding the membership of Swansea Cricket Club during the middle years of the nineteenth century, thus it has not been possible to establish exactly when James Livingston joined the organisation. However, given his interest in healthy sport, it is reasonable to assume that he became involved soon after he arrived in the town. We can confirm that he was a general committee member during the period 1866-71,[1] which suggests that he had been in membership for some time before that. To support this assumption there is the evidence of later years, when Livingston played a leading role in the development and administration of cricket, football and athletics in his adopted town. Without active participation in the lives of these clubs, it is unlikely that he would have reached positions of such seniority in their administration.

Judging by the records we have, it appears that Livingston himself was no more than an average cricketer, that he did not play rugby – at least for Swansea's first fifteen – but that he was a runner of more than average calibre. Furthermore, there is considerable evidence to suggest that he maintained his fitness throughout most of his life. For example, at the age of fifty he was reported as having run a 'foot race' against a local champion, Charles Forrester, who gave the older man ten yards start in a 120-yard handicap. The first race ended in a dead heat and, as the *Cambrian* put it, 'the old man won the rerun'. Then, even at the age of 72, in 1903, he told a *Leader* reporter that he felt confident that he could run a hundred yards within ten yards of his best sprinting performance in his younger days. His principal activity with the town's athletic club, however, was as an official and, for many years, almost until the time of his death, he was the starter for all the main meetings.

Regarding cricket, the Swansea club's minute book records that Livingston was elected to its general committee in March 1867, attracting the second highest number of votes in the process. Prior to that, however, in December of the previous year, he was co-opted onto a special Field Committee, which was given the task of finding a permanent home for the cricketers. As it turned out, that proved to be a long and complex search. In the interim, the special group had to ensure the availability of the club's existing home, the Bryn-y-môr Field, which, with fashionable Swansea developing to the west, was attracting the attention of house builders. Nonetheless, the cricketers proved to be successful in their negotiations with the current tenant, a Mrs. Pugh, though they were obliged to agree to certain conditions: a stream which ran across the property had to be diverted, and the lady would need to obtain the permission of the owner. In due course agreement was reached in time for the 1868 season, but only after some hard bargaining.

Before that negotiation took place, the name Livingston was to the fore in the cricket club when, early in the 1867 season, he was given the honour of selecting an eleven to challenge that of his friend, John Llewelyn in a match at the Bryn-y-môr Field. Livingston's men batted first and their innings closed at 258 (young Billy Bancroft scoring 24). Llewelyn's side replied with a mere 105, giving Livingston's eleven a comfortable victory. According to the *Cambrian* report, however, there were extenuating circumstances, which adversely affected the innings of the defeated team. The journalist concerned reported that 'the batting of the winning side was splendid', but felt it necessary to add 'but it was a poor ground', implying that Livingston's eleven had enjoyed an advantage. Presumably the state of the wicket would have been a topic of conversation at the end of the match, as it has been with cricketers since time immemorial. Consequently, particularly having in mind Livingston's role in the Field Committee, it is highly likely that the post-match discussion between players and officials provided the *Cambrian* journalist with a clear insight. He ended his report with the words:

> It seems strange that the corporation, with such means at its disposal, does not make some provision for healthful recreation of the inhabitants of the town. All available ground is being rapidly built upon. Why not, therefore, at once secure those fields near the turnpike and Mumbles Road (from Gorse Lane to Brynmill Terrace) for the purpose of a people's park?

The penny was to take some time to drop, however.

Llewelyn and Livingston, having been present throughout the day, would have been involved in the discussion, which suggests that the seeds sown then would have had an influence on the 'battle for the open spaces', which, in due course, another Llewelyn associate, William Thomas of Lan, would lead. Certainly, the idea appealed to the cricketers of that time for, as E. W. Jones records regarding Bryn-y-môr, 'in those days football was played over the cricket pitch and consequently . . . given fine weather, the wickets were never at any time fit to play on.'[2] At the proposed ground there would be space to obviate that problem. The immediate action of the Field Committee was to visit Colonel Morgan to establish whether he would sub-let a portion of the land at St. Helen's to the cricketers. With several house builders attempting to reach agreement with him, the colonel's answer was a firm no! Time, however, coupled with the activities of Thomas of Lan and his cohorts, was to work in favour of the cricketers. Six years later, on being given notice to quit the Bryn-y-môr Field, together with the footballers, they vigorously pursued the idea of developing a new ground at St. Helen's. Happily, Livingston and Llewelyn, who were the key figures in the negotiation, succeeded in obtaining a short lease for the very property which the *Cambrian* man had mentioned. Thus it was that Swansea's new Cricket Field was opened with the club's annual athletics meeting on Whit Monday 1875.

In February 1876, at the annual meeting of the cricket club, James Livingston was elected vice-president in formal recognition of the effective work which he had undertaken on behalf of the club; the president was John Llewelyn. Unbeknown to them at the time, both men would be involved in the near future with Thomas of Lan in saving the the new ground from the developers. All three men shared the same philosophy regarding healthful activity for the working man; it was that bond, reinforced by astute use of local press, together with influential individuals and organisations in the town which, in the end, ensured victory for the 'open-spacers'. However, it turned out to be a long-drawn-out battle.

By 1878 the controversy regarding the future of the new ground had still not been resolved. The land involved was actually owned by the corporation but had been leased to Colonel Morgan, whose executors wished to drive a road through the grounds as a prelude to the development of an estate of dwelling houses. Not surprisingly, the cricketers, footballers and athletes who used the field were less than enamoured with the idea of having to leave, particularly after spending a considerable amount of money and time in developing it. They were fortunate, then, to have such a formidable trio fighting the battle on their behalf. Quite rightly, Thomas of Lan has been recognised in the history of Swansea as the prime mover in the 'open-spaces' movement, but he was greatly assisted by the patronage of John Llewelyn and the able collaboration of James Livingston, particularly with regard to the matter of the Cricket Field. The developers and those who supported them declared that, in return for surrendering the lease to the new ground, they wanted £10,000, while the corporation said that they did not have the money. That led to an impasse, and the controversy rumbled on for some time. Indeed, it was not until 1885 that the matter was finally put to rest, after Thomas of Lan, Llewelyn and others had contributed substantial sums of money to a fund set up for the purpose of saving the new Cricket Field. It was a measure of the quality of Livingston's part in the victory and his standing in the three clubs which used St. Helen's, that he was elected as one of two trustees (the other was John Llewelyn) who were to have oversight of the hard-won lease document. In addition, the two men were the authorized signatories for the New Field bank account. Livingston, was unswerving in his belief in the importance of healthy, physical activity and the necessity of providing adequate facilities so that the working man might participate. Coupled with his successful record of service to the three sporting organisations, he was perceived as being the ideal man for the role of trustee, hence his appointment. Many years later, however, some were to take a different view of the man, for by then, they wanted to restrict the use of the Cricket Field to the two main clubs.

Meanwhile, thanks to the devoted attention paid by groundsman John Tucker to the establishment and care of a fine playing surface, it developed, both for rugby and cricket to the extent that the Cricket Field was generally recognised as having the best surface in the country. Llewelyn and Livingston took full advantage of this to attract such famous figures as W. G. Grace, Lillywhite and the 'Demon Bowler' Spoforth, to play at the ground, much to the delight of cricket lovers in the town. Nevertheless, in 1901 Livingston expressed his frustration with the committee of Glamorgan Cricket Club. At the annual meeting of Swansea Cricket and Football Club, he proposed that a resolution be sent to the county club to the effect that, unless the county eleven were seen more frequently at

St. Helen's, the Swansea club's support would be withdrawn. Livingston stated that no Swansea representative had been invited to a Glamorgan meeting for the last two years. He had made telephonic contact with Mr Brain on several occasions to protest about the lack of games at St. Helen's, but the chairman had told him that county clubs would not come to Swansea. That, he thought was 'bosh'. It would appear that the 'it's not only for Cardiff but for the whole of Wales' philosophy was as alive and well at the turn of the twentieth century as it is at the time of writing.

In continuing his crusade to encourage people to look after their bodies, Livingston took every opportunity open to him. He was particularly prominent in that respect with regard to alcohol, but the tobacco manufacturers provided him with another target. In an age when smoking was widespread and when there was little pressure on the cigarette makers from any health lobby, Livingston illustrated an unusual awareness of the potential problems which stemmed from tobacco usage. In all probability his insight was based on his experience with athletes and footballers and there is evidence that he encouraged those with whom he came into contact, to give up, or at least suspend the habit. He did not stop there however. As chairman of a Gospel Temperance meeting in October 1884, called to encourage people to support the Blue Ribbon Savings Bank, he used the opportunity to kill two birds with one stone. 'I wonder if I could get any of you gentlemen to give up your smoking', he asked. This provoked laughter from the audience and loud 'hear hears' from the ladies, allowing Livingston to make another personal statement in a helpful atmosphere. His first suggestion was that the smokers might start by reducing their consumption of tobacco, though he made no secret of the fact that he believed in giving up the habit completely. He told his audience that he had done so and felt that much better because of it. Then, linking neatly with the theme of the evening, he illustrated the financial benefits which were the result of his decision. He had made a calculation of the cost of smoking five cigars a

James Livingston – 'Local personality and golfer'.

day: at 4d. each, this amounted to £30 per year, which, over the twenty years he had been smoking, cost him £600. Then, no doubt with an eye on guilt as a motivator, he announced that he was 'perfectly ashamed' that, over twenty years he had wasted so much money in smoke. Whilst few members of his audience could relate their experience to such sums, the principle was clear, and it is reasonable to assume that some of the seeds of his advice found fertile ground. Disappointingly, however, if we are to judge by a *Leader* cartoon, reproduced on page 92, he had fallen by the wayside himself for, as will be seen, he is shown with a cigar in hand. Livingston had been successful in persuading most of the footballers of the Swansea club to at least reduce the amount they smoked. Apart from the negative effect on breathing, it was one factor which could be monitored reasonably easily, allowing the captain to remind any transgressor of the consequences.

The influence of James Livingston on the development of the rugby football section of the Swansea club and the breadth of his reputation for that work, was demonstrated in 1910. At that point, although a Dissenter who had publicly 'crossed swords' with the Established Church, he was invited to contribute an article on rugby for a special booklet published to raise funds to build a new vicarage for the Sketty parish.[3] He must have had, or known where to find, the Swansea club's records, too, for he listed in the item the first team to represent the All Whites at the rugby game. Over his lifetime, his dedication to the work which he undertook on behalf of the rugby footballers of his adopted town is amply demonstrated by many press reports. Judging by this and other evidence, it appears that, for many years, he was the *de facto* leader of the organisation, and was held in great esteem by the players.

For example, at the end of a very successful 1889-90 season, it was Livingston who, at a special dinner at the Mackworth Hotel, spoke in glowing terms of the team and its 'unparalleled captain', William Bowen. His influence, too, was demonstrated at the same event when the club secretary emphasised the level of commitment of the players: 'they had trained hard, and excess in all things had been carefully avoided'. It might have been Livingston himself speaking. He was also to the fore when everything seemed to be going wrong at the club. At the 1892 annual meeting, for example, following an indifferent season which was exacerbated by the spectre of the Northern Union which had begun to spread its shadow over the Cricket Field, the press detected an air of despondency at the club. At a closed meeting, Livingston reminded his audience of the excellent results of recent years. He urged them to think positively, and attempted to defuse the rumour which was circulating about the James brothers going north. He left his listeners in no doubt that he abhorred the professional scouts who were making their presence felt in the town. He spoke of the 'snares, dangers and disappointments of professionalism under the Northern Union' and urged Swansea men to turn their backs on these advances. He was well aware of the appeal of the northern silver to the ordinary working man and the dangers to the standing of the Swansea club if the better men were enticed away. So, apart from his stirring orations, he needed something concrete to help him in his fight. To meet this need, he conceived of the idea of the club visiting Paris and playing a match there. At that time few, if any of the players had ever crossed the channel, and consequently, they viewed the prospect of such a trip with relish. As one of the players put it when talking to the press, 'it was a bit like a posh Sunday school outing'.

Using his many contacts in Paris, Livingston arranged the trip during which the 'All Whites' played an 'All France XV'. Stade Française were to have been the opponents but, in keeping with the Swansea club's reputation, the French authorities asked if they could field a stronger representative side. The trip proved to be a great success; Swansea were victorious on the pitch, the experience was greatly appreciated by the players and there was evidence of what present-day sports psychologists would call greater 'squad bonding'. Whatever advantages Livingston saw in that activity, he was well aware of the potential benefits which might stem from it in the fight against the 'northern poachers'. It was, as it were, a positive deterent.

In 1899 Livingston revealed another aspect of his business vision for Swansea Rugby Club. As he saw things, not only were the northern poachers a continuing threat to the club and game, so was the growing danger of soccer, which was becoming popular in Swansea schools. Like many rugby administrators of that time he saw soccer, with its professional base in the big conurbations in England, as being detrimental to the oval-ball game. In line with the 'open space' philosophy which was a fundamental principle underlying the establishment of what was now referred to by some as St. Helen's, a number of soccer games were permitted on the ground, including some which involved professionals. Livingston argued against allowing that, saying that the open space was for the amateur, be he working man, middle-class or gentry. The outcome of this thinking was the presentation of a 'valuable cup for which rugby teams from Swansea schools might compete' (thus discouraging soccer). If the round-ball men wanted to bring the professional game to the town they would have to find their own stadium. In due course Livingston was to take a slightly different view of soccer – as long as it was of the amateur variety.

Season 1899/1900 proved to be another successful campaign for Swansea rugby. For the second season in succession the 'Whites' were champions, losing just once in a programme of thirty-two matches.[4] This prompted the club's president, John Llewelyn, to give a banquet in celebration at the Metropole Hotel. He was the first to speak after dinner, and, after praising the players for their efforts, went on to say that 'Mr Livingston, Mr C. H. Perkins and myself might not have been here tonight if we hadn't taken care of our bodies'. When James Livingston rose, he spoke glowingly of the president's sportsmanlike qualities and of his efforts to save St. Helen's from the developers. His play on words to conclude his speech were approved by all. Llewelyn, he said was 'a president without precedent', which brought forth loud applause from the gathered throng.

The 'All Whites' versus the Barbarians, 1905, St. Helen's.

Two years later, Livingston, with the club having lost the James brothers and others to the Northern Union, was faced with the news that a former Swansea player, McCutcheon, had been seen in the town trying to recruit players for a northern side. Angry at a man he called a traitor, Livingston was vehement in his condemnation of the individual: 'The man should be thrown into the North Dock, tarred and feathered, put in a barrel and sent back home'. Then he spoke of 'traitor's silver' and cited the case of the James brothers in order to emphasise the danger of joining 'the enemy'. Referring to them, he told his audience 'one was engaged, one fell ill . . . they were both discarded and came back to Swansea. It was a good job that the club helped, otherwise Evan James's widow would have died of starvation'. While these comments might seem to be rather melodramatic today, as can be seen from other sections of this book, those wishing to influence thinking during this period of Swansea's history must have found a certain element of hyperbole to be acceptable in ensuring that their message would find its mark.

It was in 1906, when Livingston was seventy-five, that a dispute arose which signalled the beginning of the end of his long and close association with Swansea Cricket and Football Club. As has been mentioned, certain factions within the club's general committee, perhaps understandably jealous of their world-renowned facility, wished to take measures to prevent its over-use. Livingston saw this as being contrary to the fundamental principles behind the hard-won lease, which he was holding on behalf of the clubs, and spoke against the proposed restrictions. When the committee persisted, he refused to release the lease document, which provoked them to threaten him with legal action in order to retrieve it. His response was typically obdurate; he informed the committee that he intended to fight on behalf of the Swansea Schools League and the amateur athletic clubs, which should, he argued, be allowed to use St. Helen's on the same conditions as the town's cricket and football clubs. Eventually a compromise was agreed, but not before Livingston, a man who had given so much time, energy and money to the senior clubs over many years, had failed to obtain re-election as vice-president of the cricket and football club. He had been involved in senior office there for almost forty years and, as will have been noted from this brief summary of that association, he had made a significant and effective contribution to its life throughout that time.

This unhappy episode was, unfortunately, a second blow to James

Livingston. In addition to his membership of the St. Helen's board, he had served for fifteen years as a board member of the Welsh Rugby Union. In 1906 he was Swansea's only representative on that body, but failed to be re-elected at the union's annual meeting. The *Cambrian* reported this under the headline 'A sensational incident'. Four vice-presidents had been nominated for re-election and only Livingston failed to gain sufficient votes. The Swansea paper argued that this was 'an indication of the increasing degree to which the board is passing under Rhondda control'. Yet, according to the *Cambrian*, Livingston was the only man of standing from the four top Welsh teams who had argued for the senior clubs to allow fixtures with Rhondda clubs. It was ironic, therefore, that in hitting back at the big clubs, they had made James Livingston the sacrificial lamb. 'Feelings locally', the *Cambrian* reported, 'are embittered at the moment . . . Now Swansea, the premier team in the four kingdoms, one which has done more than any other to fill the coffers of the union is . . . unrepresented on the board'. Livingston called it a dirty business. He said that he had been travelling for two months and was away when the coup occurred. 'For many years', he continued 'the club [i.e. the Welsh Union] existed on the good nature of Swansea'. He agreed that he had given a 'sort of promise' to retire, but had been urged by the Swansea committee to 'go in again'. The outcome was not what had been expected and there was no doubt that Livingston had been hurt in the process. Furthermore, the St. Helen's men who had persuaded him to stand again were extremely unhappy with the outcome.

Reading between the lines of these and other press reports of the two incidents, it would appear that they soured Livingston's view of rugby administration in Wales. Together with the difficulties which he was facing in other fields of his activity at around the same time, it must have made him wonder about continuing with his active life of service to his fellow man. He would not have been human if he had not thought of retiring quietly. Yet, whilst all leopards may have difficulty in changing their spots, old ones find the process to be even more painful. Service was a way of life for James Livingston. Even though rejected by organisations which should have been lastingly grateful for his years of loyal and effective service, there were other paths for the ageing patriarch to follow.

It would be unfair to conclude this chapter on a negative note. Notwithstanding the two unhappy episodes discussed above, his record as an

Cycle racing at St. Helen's, c.1890.

effective administrator in many fields of healthful activity stands for itself. Apart from the several activities discussed in this chapter, Livingston gave his support to many organisations. For example, those related to Swansea Workingmen's Club are dealt with in Chapter 6 as are those of the Swansea YMCA. In addition, he was involved with the Welsh Racing Cyclists' Association, the Swansea Amateur Swimming Club, the athletics and bicycle sports at St. Helen's, the Cambrian Rowing Club, Swansea Harriers Athletic Club, the Swansea Cricket League, and the Chamber of Commerce road walk to Llandeilo. No doubt, there were others too, for over all, it is fair to say that during his working lifetime, Livingston's contribution to the promotion, organisation and administration of healthy recreation for the men of Swansea was unparalleled. So much so, indeed, that had he done nothing else for his fellow man, the part that he played in the sporting life of the town should have been sufficient to ensure his place in Swansea's annals.

REFERENCES

1. Swansea Cricket Club. *Minute Book*, 1866-1871.
2. E. W. Jones 'Recollections of Twenty Years' South Wales Cricket', in *St Paul's Church, Sketty; A Souvenir.* Sketty: The church, 1910; pp. 50-2.
3. James Livingston, 'Football', in *St. Paul's, Sketty*, 1910, supra, pp. 22-4.
4. David Farmer, *The All Whites*, op. cit., pp. 57-61.

CHAPTER 4

Temperance

Kenneth O. Morgan, in his book: *Rebirth of a Nation: Wales 1880-1890*, describes the interaction between nonconformity and the temperance movement as 'ferociously zealous',[1] and it is probable that observers of the activities of James Livingston and his colleagues during the latter half of the nineteenth century would have agreed with this contention. Theirs was a crusade, for to them, alcoholic drink was as evil as were those who distributed it. As they saw it, brewers, distillers and the landlords, all collaborated to take hard-earned money from often uneducated workers, whilst causing misery to their families and damaging their health. From their perspective they saw the financially and politically powerful 'drink trade' as a wicked enemy.

Faced with such formidable opponents, the leaders of the temperance movement realised that, if they were to influence the situation, they needed to muster and deploy their resources in the most effective way. Since their own financial power was extremely limited when compared with that of the brewers, the movement had to develop a strategy which made the most of their strength. When they assessed their position, it became clear that they had to win the support of the masses and, where better to recruit members than from the fertile ground of the Dissenting chapels? It was the 'Army of Right' which emerged from this recognition that James Livingston and others were to lead in Swansea during the second half of the nineteenth century.

At the time Livingston came to Swansea, the drink trade was well-established in the town, and public houses and small beer-houses abounded. As had happened in most of the towns and cities around the country, the brewers placed their outlets in the most advantageous locations. For example, public houses were established near the gates of the works in Landore where men toiled all day in the heat of furnaces and, in the process, lost body fluid. Not surprisingly, many men, thirsty at the end of their shifts, took advantage of the public house. Then, having walked home, they could usually find another hostelry nearby. It was a powerful and successful formula for business success, but one which was paid for, the temperance leaders argued, by the resultant misery and ill-health of the working population and their families, and by the disruption of society. Between 1869 and 1873, for example, drunkenness in Swansea almost trebled and, for the latter half of that period, one person in seventy-four was convicted of being drunk.[2]

It was against this background that James Livingston started his temperance work, probably on joining Wesley Chapel in Goat Street, Swansea, during the 1850s. In one respect he was an unlikely champion for the cause, since he had been educated in France where it was normal to consume wine with most meals. It is probable, too, that as a young man in Paris he had visited some of the many cafés in the city which offered alcoholic drinks, and may have consumed a variety of these in the process. However, after his arrival in Swansea, it would appear that he underwent some kind of experience which caused him to change his position on the question of drinking alcholic liquor, for, during his Swansea years he violently condemned the 'devil in the glass'. Livingston was to refer to the benefits of his 'conversion' on numerous occasions, usually in the form of a personal testimony. Whatever, or whoever it was that influenced him, it left Swansea with a remarkable champion of the temperance cause.

In the early 1860s, James Livingston was Sunday school superintendent at Wesley Chapel, which was a significant organisation. A decade earlier, J. Lewis, in his *Swansea Guide*, had noted that the school had 154 scholars and twenty-five teachers.[3] Taking into consideration the religious climate in Swansea at the time Livingston was appointed to the post of superintendent, it is highly likely that the numbers involved were at least as large. Because this was so, Livingston's role was extremely important in the life of the chapel. Its leaders had selected him, presumably, because of his personal qualities, but also because he was young enough to appeal to a broad range of youngsters, and yet old enough to satisfy parents that their children were in safe hands. During this period the Blue Ribbon movement was growing nationwide, as were other temperance organisations like the Band of Hope, and the Gospel Temperance Union. Since the Methodist Church was usually in the forefront of such work, it may be the case that Livingston either started, or continued with, a midweek temperance meeting for children and adults. Another factor which influenced the situation was the fact that, among the senior members of the Goat Street congregation, were several men who managed, or had managed, major copper works in Landore, and had seen the alcohol problem detrimentally affecting their workers. Consequently, once again, Livingston had a following wind when he began his work in the field.

At this point it is important to point out that the temperance movement was not confined to the Dissenting chapels. Both the Anglican and Catholic communities had their own organisations, which promoted at least moderation in respect of the use of alcohol. However, having in mind the subject of this book, it is inevitable that there is something of a nonconformist focus in the present discussion.

With a bigger canvas on which to work, Livingston quickly assumed the role of one of the leaders of the temperance cause in Swansea. Since there were many able champions of the movement among the Dissenting chapel population, this suggests a great deal about his abilities and charisma. Certainly, it was during this period that he began to demonstrate the zealous fervour noted by Morgan a century later. He eagerly took advantage of the significant platforms which became available to him to promote the temperance message, most often using his powers of oratory to best effect. He was single-minded, fearless and led from the front. If he had a weakness it was that his fervour led him to make statements which, in some cases, were less than measured, whilst in others caused offence or attracted criticism, for example, of class or political bias. Yet Livingston believed that he was arguing for the 'Right', and presumably, that the enthusiastic reaction of the majority of his audiences confirmed the fact that his message had a beneficial influence on their thinking.

Consequently, despite being aware of a certain amount of criticism, he continued with his approach. As irascible as ever, he spoke at a conference at Swansea's Guildhall, which had been arranged 'for the purposes of eliciting local public opinion with regard to the Local Option debate'.[4] On this occasion Livingston supported the town's mayor, Thomas Davies, on the motion 'This conference is deeply impressed with the importance of temperance legislation ... and strongly urges the government to give a Local Option bill to Wales'. Since this was a Liberal proposal, Livingston had nailed his political colours to the mast. That flag was to fly at temperance meetings on many future occasions. In itself that might not have created too many problems. However, as will be seen, from time to time, matters were exacerbated by Livingston's zeal, a characteristic which caused him to be less than sensitive about the feelings of some of the people who crossed his path during his campaigning and who held different views from his own.

Meanwhile, no stone was left unturned in the search for ever-wider support and commitment to the temperance cause. Like their Salvation Army brethren, the Dissenters used poetry, music and drama to enhance their message. Around this time it seems that Livingston appeared on the platform, chaired the meeting or spoke at the majority of major gatherings of temperance people in Swansea. He was in the chair at one meeting in 1885 where the Blue Ribbon Choir was reported as having 'rendered an anthem and the drunkard's soliloquy', and, on rising to speak he was 'received with great applause'. Warming to his reception, Livingston was as expansive as ever. His opening sentence set the scene. Referring to the discussion concerning the Local Option Bill, which was imminently expected in Parliament, he said that he was of the opinion that 'there was never a time in the history of the world more marked by universal commotion than the present'. He argued that statesmen were seeking solutions 'too far from home', which meant that temperance people had a duty to 'bring home to both parties what we consider to be the great question of the day (applause)'. He told his audience that they should question candidates in the coming election about their position on this matter. He believed that there were 'two distinct sides: the Temperance Party and the Liquor Party, and the question is, who will give the people the power to keep evil from their homes?' It was not a question of Mr Dillwyn or Mr Meredyth, the local candidates at the approaching general election, 'but who will fail to answer a straight question: who is for temperance and who for liquor?' For Livingston it was either black or white; weasel words would not suffice. Having brought temperance into the political arena, his next step was to invoke the Lord. 'Whoever is elected,' he continued,' will be in power, so may God help them to do so rightly (loud cheers and applause)'.

Just in case anyone had not perceived which party was on the Lord's side that day, at a further Blue Ribbon meeting in the following month, Mr Dillwyn was chairman and was supported by James Livingston and another doughty fighter for the temperance cause, Dr John Adams

Rawlings. Livingston wasted little time in making his position clear. What Swansea needed, he said, was 'a man who will support the righteous cause (loud cheers)'. It was clear, he continued, that Mr Dillwyn had been a staunch supporter of the temperance cause, whereas it was just as obvious which group would favour Mr Meredyth, and he them. According to Livingston, '99 publicans out of 100 will support Mr Meredyth'. The question was 'should they [the electors] support that body or should they support Mr Dillwyn?' The volume of cheers and applause answered the question, at least as far as the majority of people present at that meeting were concerned.

In June 1888 the *Cambrian* published a letter from a correspondent who signed himself 'Temperance', a pseudonym which, if we are to judge by the content of the missive, implied more than simply relating to alcohol. It was a letter critical of James Livingston's all-embracing approach to speaking and chairing a meeting which was held under the auspices of the Gospel Temperance Union at the Albert Hall. Temperance felt that Livingston's address 'did not seem to be entirely devoted to the propagation of the Gospel of Temperance'. In addition, he thought that 'a suspicion was aroused that political topics of a Radical tendency were not excluded from the programme.' Furthermore, continued Temperance, 'Mr Livingston brought up a religious question . . . one that can never be raised without exciting embittered feelings . . . and proceeded to deal with that question controversially as it presents itself to the view of the individual Protestant Dissenter'. The letter-writer also complained that the chairman had abused his position by 'assuming the role of ecclesiastical gladiator, and, in a fit of jingoism, at once puritanic and quixotic, dealt with the matter very heavily'.

Knowing something of Livingston's tendencies, a neutral observer would have found Temperance's letter to be reasonable criticism, couched as it was in unprovocative language. Livingston, however, was prone to be somewhat insensitive about the effects of his forthright views on people whose ideas differed from his own. Presumably he believed that he could win many more people to the temperance cause by continuing with his approach, than would be offended by what he said or by the way in which he made his case. This was again an instance of the end justifying the means.

Certainly, Temperance had a sound case with respect to one sweeping generalisation made by Livingston during that Albert Hall meeting. He foresaw a changing political scene in the United Kingdom, and according to him 'the strength and power of the world is to be found in the masses, for any movement for the good comes from there'. At this distance one wonders what his friends, Sir John Llewelyn and the Grenfells, felt about his assertion, for both had shared temperance platforms with him, while the largesse which the two families had shown in Swansea over a long period indicated a caring concern for ordinary people by those members of the town's gentry. Once more, Livingston was painting his world with a nine-inch paddle brush. It was the quickest way to complete the wall, even if the finish was not always perfect!

Whilst he enjoyed the big stage, in many respects he was more at home with smaller groups of people, such as the members of a Ragged School temperance meeting in January 1895. The chairman for the evening told him that 150 men, women and children had signed the pledge during the previous twelve months. Livingston expressed his delight at this, which, he said, was a real achievement and one which demonstrated the hard work of the school's leaders. He was moved, he continued, 'by the sincerity of those to whom I have spoken'. It could not have been a better cue, for he launched into his testimony with obvious passion. 'I have had a spirit of thankfulness during the last ten years that I am alive, and the deepest conviction that, if I had not stopped drinking I should not be alive now (cheers)'. Whilst the words were dramatic and open to scientific challenge, it was his mode of address: clear, firm, sincere and intelligible, which captured the attention of his audience. It would have been difficult to find another role model who could have communicated in that environment as effectively as did James Livingston.

Later that month, as if to underscore Livingston's assertions about the 'Army of Right', the two distinct parties, Temperance and Liquor, and good only coming from the masses, Lord Randolph Churchill introduced a bill in Parliament in response to which the temperance leaders called a meeting at Swansea's Guildhall. It was a well-attended gathering and Livingston was quickly into his stride. A better example of landed gentry than Churchill would have been difficult to find, and in Livingston's view His Lordship's action was 'an indication of the crisis which is facing the country.' According to him, 'No political, theological or international matter of greater importance has been placed before Parliament during the last five hundred years' – which would be regarded by most people as overstating his case more than somewhat. The issue involved related to the potential compensation which would have to be paid to publicans when 'sensible men decide to reduce the number of public houses' in their area. 'Our town', he continued, 'will have to pay thousands of pounds to these purveyors of the evil drink'. In his most forthright platform manner, raising his papers in his hand he declaimed, to long and loud applause, 'We will not have it!'

To conclude this chapter, it should be stressed that the foregoing discussion is but illustrative of James Livingston's lasting passion for the temperance cause. For example, he was a fervent supporter of the developments which led to the passing of the Welsh Sunday Closing act of 1881.[5] If anyone personified Morgan's 'ferocious zeal', it was he, and it was zeal which characterised him to the end of his life. Throughout the time he spent in Swansea he was a tireless worker for temperance and, judging by the contemporary press, he influenced thousands of people to sign the pledge and work for the 'Army of Right'. He and his colleagues, including his friend, Dr. J. Adams Rawlings, created and nurtured a formidable anti-drink ethos, which was to retain its influence in Swansea up to the middle of the twentieth century.[6] Despite the financial and political power of the liquor lobby and, notwithstanding his inclination to resort to hyperbole and his tendency to speak his mind, Livingston's achievements as a leader of the temperance cause in Swansea were notable. Taken by themselves these successes would have been a triumphant life-time's experience for any one individual. When they are considered in conjunction with Livingston's very many other interests and activities they may be seen to have been even more remarkable.

REFERENCES

1. Morgan, op. cit., p. 17.
2. W. R. Lambert, *Drink and Sobriety in Victorian Wales*. Cardiff: University of Wales Press, 1983, p. 47.
3. Lewis, op. cit., p. 22.
4. The ideas behind the Local Option Bill of 1885 originated in 1853 from a group of Manchester men who called themselves the UK Alliance. A year after the formation of this organisation, a brewer, Charles Burton, published a paper entitled 'How to stop drunkenness', which summarised the group's thinking, and, in 1857, the Carlisle Liberal MP, Wilfred Lawson, introduced a bill to the House of Commons which embodied the fundamental ideas outlined in Burton's paper. There was one important difference, however, for the bill did not advocate total prohibition. Instead it provided

that, on application, the ratepayers in any district (parish, township or borough) could vote on the question of whether the liquor traffic should exist in that district or not, a majority of two thirds of those voting being necessary to decide. In Wales, following the successful adoption of the Sunday Closing Act of 1881, there was a significant lobby in favour of a Welsh version of the Local Option Bill. Such a bill was introduced by Bowen Rowlands in 1887, but it failed to gain adoption at that time and on two further occasions, the last of which was in 1891.
5. The Welsh Sunday Closing Act, 1881, was a legislative landmark in that it was the first distinctly Welsh Act of Parliament.
6. G. P. Neilson 'Dr John Adam Rawlings (1848-1933)', *Minerva*, Vol. 8 (2000), pp. 27-36.

CHAPTER 5

The Wesleyan Connection and Family Life

Wesley Chapel, which James Livingston joined on coming to Swansea, was a flourishing Christian community. Rejoicing in a membership of almost six hundred, and a Sunday school of 154 pupils, it was one of the largest nonconformist places of worship in the town.[1] Given these statistics, it is reasonable to conclude that, at the same time, there was also a strong young people's fellowship in the chapel. If that were so, it would have been one of the factors which appealed to a young bachelor (Livingston was twenty-four at the time) seeking to join a place of worship and wishing to become involved in a social environment which had a Christian ethos. Another influence in bringing him to Wesley was, probably, his school friend, Thomas Cory. The Cory family of Cardiff and Swansea were devout Wesleyans and it would have been natural for a young son, brought up in the tradition of that branch of Methodism, on coming to Swansea, to seek out the leading church in that denomination. It is also possible that Thomas would have been James Livingston's sponsor in introducing his friend to the stewards and minister of Wesley Chapel. By whichever means he came to the chapel, the future was to show that Livingston's choice of a place of worship had considerable influence on his life. For example, he forged lifelong links with several prominent members of the church and shared a common ethic with them; all were motivated to serve their fellow man and help improve his lot. One of these was Frank Ash Yeo, a Cory relative by marriage, who became an MP and, like Livingston, mayor of Swansea and a JP. Another was Dr. John Adams Rawlings, with whom he worked closely over many years in the temperance movement.

Livingston, of course, was unaware of how these relationships would influence him, but there was another aspect concerning which his awareness was heightened quite early in his time at Wesley. Among the young people in the chapel was Mary Jane Brewer, the daughter of a master mariner, who lived at 9 Cleveland Terrace. She was three years younger than James and, after courting for several years, the couple were married at Wesley in April 1859 and set up home, initially at 9 Cradock Street. Three years later, the marriage was blessed with the birth of their first child, Irene. Meanwhile, Livingston had been establishing himself within Swansea's business fraternity and, by 1865, the firm of Richards and Livingston was included among the companies listed in *Pearce's and Brown's Swansea Directory* for that year. In the interim, the family had increased in number as a result of the birth of a son, Ernest and a second daughter, Beatrice. In 1868, a third daughter, Ethelwin came into the world. Sadly, however, Mary Jane was not to see her grow up, for the mother died in February of the following year. Livingston, 38 at the time, thus found himself a widower with four children. Taking account of his many and varied activities, it could not have been easy bringing up a family, although the 1871 census shows that, among those who were resident at 78 Mansel Street, were a governess and two female servants. However, since both servants (aged 28 and 34) were from Great Rudbaxton in Pembrokeshire, near Livingston's birthplace, they may well have had a closer relationship with the children of the house than might have been the norm.

During that period at Wesley, James was establishing himself among the leading figures in the chapel, and this was to become more evident as he matured. He served as a Sunday school teacher and subsequently became superintendent; he became a steward (the Methodist equivalent of a deacon or elder) and, in due course, a circuit steward. From his earliest days in the church he was associated with the temperance movement, emerging as time passed as a major figure in its work in Swansea. He was a lay preacher of some note, and was committed to that work almost to the end of his life. He was also one of the senior figures appointed to oversee the construction of the building and develop the membership of Brunswick Chapel,[2] a new Wesleyan cause near Swansea Hospital. At the time of his death, the scope of his activities was put into context by an extract from a short eulogy which appeared in the *Swansea and Gower Wesleyan Record*. The journal reported that 'he has been pretty well everything in Methodism, and it is pleasing to know that he died as a local preacher'.[3]

In 1893 a man who had been a pupil at Wesley Sunday school when James Livingston was the superintendent there gave a talk at the chapel recalling those days. Fortunately, the transcript of his presentation has survived, for it provides further insight into Livingston and the environment

Brunswick Chapel soon after opening in 1873.

within which he worked. The speaker, William Robinson, who was a boy of ten when he first joined the Sunday school at Wesley, described how he had been diffident about approaching a group of youths who were standing outside the building when he arrived for the first time. When he did speak to them, to his consternation, their attitudes and the foul language which they used were not what he had been expecting. As he put it, 'I approached these supposed gentlemen with a sickening sensation of disgust . . . the tongue maketh itself known in horrid oaths and unkind ingenuous remarks'.[4] From this and other evidence we can conclude that, at least some of the raw material with which the teachers at Wesley were working reflected the rough-and-ready nature of Swansea's labouring class at the time. These folk, most of whom were unskilled, had come to Swansea from many places, seeking jobs. Indeed, the fast developing industrial economy of the town with its melting-pot of incomers and locals, might be thought of as being a 'frontier' environment in both a religious and educational sense. Little wonder, then, that James Livingston and his colleagues at Wesley maintained a missionary outlook. Among the thousands of people who lived around the chapel and its environs there were many minds to feed and souls to save.

Among other things, Robinson's paper also provides a fascinating description of the environment in which the Sunday school was conducted. He recalled:

> It seemed a strange thing to follow down the steps to the cellar under the street . . . The thought of the grave comes coldly to mind . . . and the flickering gas jets show the walls washed with a bluish tint, giving the place a sepulchre appearance . . . The eye becomes adjusted to the queer place . . . The girls are hurrying to the side next to the windows, sitting on those backless plain forms, but still sitting in heaven's light . . . The boys . . . made for that long wall, so black that the shadows are thick.

Later in his speech, Robinson spoke warmly of James Livingston. Recalling the collective opinion of the boys of those days he argued that they regarded the superintendent as 'our Livingstone', a comparison with the explorer. In addition the boys likened him to the Italian hero Garibaldi:[5] fearless, though they thought of him as a bigger and kinder man. Such an accolade from boys with whom he had worked closely over many years speaks volumes for a dedicated teacher, and this despite the fact that Livingston had his own problems for, being a widower with four children, he must have found family life somewhat difficult. So, it was not surprising, that he began courting a new lady. He had business connections in many places, Cardiff being among them, and it was during one of his visits to the eastern port that he met Amelia Latch, who was to become his second wife. Apart from the fact that she lived in a different town, there was another interesting feature about this liaison. As Grenville Neilson notes, 'not all Wesleyans were supportive of other nonconformist denominations'.[6]

Clearly, Livingston took a less inhibited stance, for his fiancée was a member of Cardiff's Charles Street Congregational Church.[7] It was in 1872 that the couple were married in the bride's church and, subsequently, settled in Swansea. Sadly, the marriage was not long-lived, for in 1878 Amelia died, following which, James was destined to remain a widower until his own death in 1912. The marriage, however, was not without issue; two further sons, Frank and Burton, were born. Consequently, when Amelia died, her husband was left with six children.

Yet Livingston carried on with his work; indeed, he appeared to be continually adding to his list of activities. One of those, which stemmed from his church life, was his involvement in the establishment of a branch of the YMCA in Swansea. This was the type of project which appealed to him, for it was focused upon young people, whom he saw as the future of society and of service to the community. In 1865 he attended a meeting of the Swansea Sunday Schools Union in the schoolroom of Castle Street Chapel, during which a resolution was passed to form a committee with the objective of establishing a YMCA in the town. This objective was achieved and Livingston became the organisation's first president. Later in the same year, Livingston was to the fore again. This time, in regard to the Wesleyan Home Mission. He acted as chairman for a fund-raising event which was held at the denomination's Mumbles chapel, and was reported as having introduced the business of the meeting with 'an excellent, concise and clever speech'. After describing the work of the mission, Livingston introduced a timeless and telling one-paragraph sermon. He said that he deplored the lack of enthusiasm among Christian people and went on to argue that 'the world generally will be slow to believe in the power of Christianity when they see its professors being lukewarm and apathetic'.

Over the years Livingston continued to promote the work of the Wesleyan Home and Foreign missions, and in 1868 he chaired the annual meeting, at the Mumbles chapel, of the local auxiliary of the two societies, which was a major source of fund-raising for missionary activities. The press reported that there was a 'large attendance and an excellent collection taken', which suggests that one of the objectives of the event was achieved. A short item in the *Leader* of 13 July 1893 demonstrates another facet of Livingston's personality. In reporting on the annual picnic of Brunswick Chapel Choir to Parkmill, the paper noted that:

> It was unanimously agreed that a great part of the happy result was due to the fact that the party was accompanied by Mr James Livingston who, as usual, kept the company in mirth and good humour throughout the day . . . and was leader in most of the outdoor games which were so heartily indulged in.

This demonstrates that there was a lighter side to the personality of the man who was a passionate fighter for so many causes. The warmth which the report records echoes that illustrated in the talk given to members at Wesley Chapel discussed earlier.[8] From this it is reasonable to conclude that he had a fine sense of humour and, despite his towering presence and his ability to lead, he must have been an approachable human being.

It was in 1891 that Livingston, who had lost two wives, had to face up to another tragedy. His youngest daughter, Ethelwin, who was only twenty-three and engaged to be married, died suddenly. A post mortem found that that she had died as a result of a clot on the brain. Whilst, like many Victorian fathers he was probably strict with his children, in the light of his extensive activities with young people, it is likely that he had a good relationship with them. Ethelwin's death was a particularly hard blow for Livingston, for as the youngest girl in the family she may well have had an even closer relationship with her father than her brothers and sisters. Nonetheless, it is indicative of her father's faith and resolve that the tragedy did not deflect him from his life's work. He continued to follow the many paths which related to his wide range of interests with undiminished dedication.

As noted in Chapter 8, in 1904, James Livingston succeeded in being re-elected to Swansea's town council, a feat which attracted plentiful comment from supporters and opponents. In the context of his chapel life, it is interesting to consider the observation of the editor of the *Swansea and Gower Wesleyan Record*, for it demonstrates that Livingston had a well-earned reputation as a doughty fighter for a worthy cause. After congratulating the patriarch on getting re-elected, the editor wrote: 'He will feel like an old war horse visiting the scene of some former conflict'.[9] The editor was to be proved right, although he might justifiably have used the plural form – conflicts. Nevertheless, the ageing process hardly appeared to touch the old warrior. In 1908, for example, whilst serving as a councillor in sometimes less than friendly circumstances, he was 'on duty' in every field of his interest. By this time his enemies were more numerous as he carried on with his various campaigns in his inimitable manner, scorning popularity in his constant search for what was right for Swansea. He seemed to be immune to the verbal barbs of those with whom he was less than popular. In particular he let nothing interfere with his chapel activities and those related to them. In the summer of 1908, for instance, following his YMCA connection, he was the prominent figure at the association's annual fête which was held at Ffynone House. In closing the event, he made a witty speech in which he thanked his host for allowing the garden to be used, the people who had made all the arrangements and had managed the affair, and those who had come to support the YMCA. He also pleased the family's gardeners when he said that, in his opinion 'Eden of old could hardly have been superior to Ffynone this afternoon'.

Leaving aside his attendance at morning and evening services each Sunday (when he was not leading a service himself), his support each Sunday afternoon of Sunday school activities at Brunswick, and regular attendance at the chapel's mid-week service, Livingston was also involved with other organisations there. As has been shown, these included temperance and missionary events, but he was also involved with debating societies in Wesley Chapel, and with youth work, and was prominent in the Brotherhood meetings which were an important part of Wesley's activities (even though he was in membership at Brunswick). In the same year as the YMCA event at Ffynone, for example, he chaired a similar meeting at the Goat Street chapel when the speaker was his colleague, Dr. J. Adams Rawlings , JP. The doctor, who was chairman of the town's Watch Committee, spoke on 'A clean Swansea', and it was Livingston who proposed the vote of thanks at the end of the evening, claiming that the speaker was 'Swansea's best friend'.

The foregoing illustrations are merely examples of the service, which James Livingston gave to his chapel. His remarkable capacity for giving himself in service in this aspect of his life is formidable enough. Yet, as argued elsewhere in this book, when his activities in the wider society of Swansea are also taken into consideration, his dedication may be seen in an even more favourable light. It seems to us that his gargantuan work-load could only have been sustained because of his inner drive, which was so clearly based upon an unchallengable belief in the word of his Lord and Saviour. That he was a nonconformist is not in doubt, nor is the fact that he had a deeply held suspicion of both the Anglican and Catholic churches. However, it is important to remember that in the context of his time, such an attitude was probably typical of the members of the various nonconformist churches, the Established Church and the Roman, *vis-à-vis* one another.

From a chapel viewpoint, the eulogy with which this chapter is concluded is indicative of what the people with whom he worked for almost fifty years at Wesley, Brunswick and in the Gower and Swansea Methodist Circuit (Mumbles, Landore, and Sketty,for example) thought of him. Again, it adds to our understanding of a truly remarkable man: 'Mr Livingston belonged to a generation of Wesley men who are now all gone to their rest. By his death the landmark disappears . . . He was a man of many parts. He had an affectionate regard for the welfare of young people. As Sunday school superintendent he was a great success and was able to raise the school to a high standard'.[10]

REFERENCES

1. Religious Census, Municipal Borough of Swansea, 28 March 1884.
2. *Brunswick Wesleyan Chapel 1873-1923: Jubilee Souvenir*, The Chapel 1923, p. 14.
3. *Swansea and Gower Wesleyan Record* (Jan./Feb. 1912).
4. William Robinson: Transcript of a talk given at Wesley during 1893. Swansea and Gower Wesleyan Church Archive, The Library, University of Wales, Swansea.
5. Giuseppe Garibaldi (1807-82) was an Italian patriot and the colourful stories which circulated about his exploits touched a chord with those seeking home rule and land reform for Wales. Consequently he became a cult figure in the principality, was adopted by the *Cymru Fydd* movement (Wales of the future), and became revered in many Welsh homes, particularly during the decade after his death. See T. Gwyn Griffiths, *Garibaldi, Cymru Fydd a Dante*, [Swansea]: Coleg y Brifysgol Abertawe, 1985.
6. G. P. Neilson, 'Dr. John Adams Rawlings', *Minerva*, Vol. 8, 2000.
7. The Charles Street Congregational building is still in existence, but is now Ebenezer Welsh Independent Church, the Congregationalists having vacated it on merging with other chapels. See: Jill Hutt, *The Churches of Charles Street,* Cardiff: Charles Street Arts,1991.
8. Robinson, op. cit.
9. *The Swansea and Gower Wesleyan Record* (Oct. 1904).
10. Ibid. (Jan./Feb. 1912).

CHAPTER 6

The Workingmen's Club and the YMCA

The Swansea Workingmen's Club and Institute was founded in 1874 by what was described as a body of energetic local men under the leadership of the Reverend G. H. Vance, the minister of the town's Unitarian Church. In his travels, Vance had seen the concept upon which the club was based working in other towns, and believed that such an institution would be of great benefit to Swansea. In order to establish the organisation on a proper footing, Vance and his colleagues had a great deal to do. Among other things, the concept required the participation of people from the various strata in Swansea society, so they had to persuade 'officers' and 'men' that they could meet on common ground – a radical concept for the time. That Vance was successful in this aspect of his mission is illustrated by a report in the *Cambrian* in March 1878 in which a journalist described the environment within which this unusual liaison occurred. 'The club', he noted, 'affords a common platform upon which the magistrate, county gentleman, merchant and higher-class trades people may meet and mingle with their artisan brethren to the mutual advantage of all concerned.'[1] With Lord Aberdare as president, a healthy representation of gentry, and a membership of several hundred artisans, all gathered in a matter of weeks, the concept quickly became a reality. It will not come as a surprise to the reader to learn that among the first people to be approached by Vance was James Livingston and, in typical fashion, the Wesleyan became involved with the new club early in 1875. It was a project which appealed to him because it provided another market segment, as it were, in which he might work to influence and benefit the working man. For example, the concept of the club included a focus on the physical well-being of members, on developing their talents through sport and exercise, and on improving their minds through lectures, discussions, reading and debate. There was also the opportunity for members to gain an appreciation of the arts and to improve their performances in music, drama and concert. As illustrated elsewhere in this book, these

The Swansea Workingmen's Club building late in its life.

approaches had much in common with Livingston's own philosophy[2] and he wanted others, who were less advantaged than he was, to have the benefit of the many opportunities which, as members of the club, were open to them.

There was also another factor, which, for Livingston, was equally important. Whilst the club was to have a bar for members, he believed that its ethos would ensure that the consumption of alcohol would be limited.

The emphasis on healthy living and self-development, with the added advantage that, at the outset at least, the club did not open on Sundays, reflected that position. This line of thinking also provided Livingston with a further opportunity. Swansea Cricket and Football Club had moved from its Bryn-y-môr Field to St. Helen's and, in any event had outgrown the Uplands Hotel which had been the club's headquarters. Taken together, the timing was perfect for Livingston to persuade the cricketers and footballers that they need look no further for a suitable facility. The outcome was that the sportsmen joined the Workingmen's Club, which replaced the Uplands Hotel as the meeting place of the men from St. Helen's. Since the sides which represented Swansea at both winter and summer games were made up of people from various sections of the town's society, the arrangement beneficially measured up to several criteria. Both parties to the negotiation – the institute and the cricket and football club – gained in the process.

In July 1875 the *Cambrian* published a review of the progress of the new organisation. Referring to the 'great work it is intended to perform in our social economy' and noting that the buildings were almost completed, while a large number of members were visiting daily, the writer thought that 'the club is an accomplished fact'. However, there was a caveat. Observing the benefits which were conferred on members as a result of its establishment, the journalist wanted to know why it had not been started before, and whether there was 'a dash of truth in the statement that Swansea, the *soi-disant* greatest centre in Wales, is sadly behind the times'. Nevertheless, late or not, it was clear that the new organisation had an important part to play in the life of Victorian Swansea, and in a very short time it had a strong and active membership.

One of the earliest formal events staged by the club took place in March 1876. It took the form of a presentation to Mr Vance, the founder of the club, who had left Swansea to take up another post. James Livingston, mayor at that time, was chairman for the evening. After a number of short speeches praising the minister's initiative, J. W. Buse, the club's librarian, presented Vance with a handsome dining-room clock in a marble case, and a silver ink stand. The gifts he said 'exemplify the gratitude of members to the clergyman for helping them to improve their social and moral condition'. In closing the event, Livingston added his own tribute, concluding it with the opinion that 'there are two causes of satisfaction, which a man might feel when he has endeavoured to benefit his fellow man in a disinterested way. The first is to find that he has been successful and the second that his work has been appreciated'. The mayor believed that Vance had met both criteria.

It was during the institute's half-yearly meeting on February 1876 that another Livingston intervention was recognised. This time he was thanked for 'having the billiard table put in order and for presenting a new set of cushions at a cost of ten pounds'. This gesture was greatly appreciated, it was said, particularly because the table was one of the most frequently used pieces of equipment in the institute. After responding to the vote of thanks, the mayor took the opportunity to remind his audience of the aims and objectives of the club and the importance of their own self-development potential. He told them that their committee considered that 'it should be no small source of agreement and usefulness that the success of the institute is, to a very great extent, the result of your industry and reliance'. Samuel Smiles would have nodded in approval.

During the following summer, Livingston was to the fore again at the club and institute's first annual meeting, during which his contributions to its life were spoken of warmly. When the secretaries of the various sections of the club gave their reports, it was announced that the mayor had become the first president of the institute's cricket club. It was a post, he said in responding, which delighted him. Yet again he enthused about the success of the institution, and urged members to take every advantage of the many opportunities for self-development which it provided. In addition, he encouraged them to fill the positions which would soon become available, and make themselves better and wiser men in the process. Presumably, Livingston was reflecting on the benefits which he had obtained from serving for many years on committees. If that was so, he may have thought that there were similar developmental opportunities available to the men who served on the institute's management committee, or those who ran each of the various sections. He went on to reinforce his message by reminding his audience of the benefits which would stem from their active participation in the life of the club. The message was not new, but it was well worth repeating. Furthermore, the old adage about the clever manager wishing to work himself out of a job may well have been at the back of Livingston's mind. As he had been on several other occasions, initially he was 'hands on' and maintained that role until he felt that there were able people in place to take the organisation forward. However, he was not ready to go yet.

In July 1876, Livingston, by kind permission of John Llewelyn, arranged a picnic and sports event at the latter's Penlle'r-gaer seat, and followed that seven days later with a cricket match at the same venue. Speaking at the end of the game, after thanking their host, he said that it had been a most enjoyable day during which he had been struck by the friendly manner in which the party seemed to unite. That, he continued, had been brought about as a result of the establishment 'of your excellent institution, Swansea Workingmen's Club! (cheers)'. Rarely did Livingston miss an opportunity to reinforce the benefits of the organisation which were available to its members, and it is interesting to note that he was careful to emphasise his own philosophy in this regard. At an earlier meeting he had referred to the institute's cricket club and said that it was not his purpose to make them better players. Rather it was to assist in bringing them together in a way which would improve their fitness, social ability and enjoyment, which may be seen to be an echo of the Olympic Games philosophy about taking part being more important than winning. It would have appealed to Victorians of all stations; that Swansea audience was no different.

During the years, which followed, Livingston, in typical fashion, involved himself in many of the facets of the life of the institute. He gave lectures on a variety of topics, arranged debates and other learning opportunities, supported fund-raising projects and encouraged the appreciation of the fine arts. On one occasion, for example, he displayed his collection of photographs of large Roman antiquities and, no doubt, gave an associated lecture as a means of adding to the understanding of interested members. One factor which ensured that he maintained reasonably close links with the club for longer than might otherwise have been the case, was his parallel involvement with the town's rugby club. As we have seen, the organisations shared the same headquarters. Livingston was particularly pleased to enjoy this dual role on the occasions when the football club won cup competitions and when the triumphant teams were met at one of Swansea's railway stations and paraded through the town's streets to the Workingmen's Club. In March 1880, when the rugby men won the South Wales Football Cup for the first time, the victors were received at the institute's original premises in High Street. Then, at the end of the 1886/7 season, the cup-winning side was treated to a torch-lit procession through various Swansea streets to the handsome building in Alexandra Road which was had been designed for the institute. Although he was there for that celebration, Livingston's one regret regarding his association with the Workingmen's Club was that, due to business commitments, he was not able to be present at the ceremony to mark the opening of the new premises. Had he been there, there is little doubt that he would have had something constructive to say, for the new facility represented a significant statement as to the success of the venture. Swansea might have been late in adopting the idea, but when it did, effective management of the process from planning to implementation ensured that it was soundly established in a very short time.

The Swansea YMCA

When a committee was set up in 1865 to consider the establishment of a Swansea branch of the YMCA, James Livingston was heavily involved in the work from the outset. Indeed, it would have been surprising had he not been so, for the organisation's stated objectives might well have been written by him. These were: 'to help forward the spiritual, intellectual, social and physical well-being of young men', and, as was clear from its name, the work to ensure the achievement of these objectives was to be undertaken through an organisation with a Christian ethos. The synergy between the man and the concept could not have been bettered, which probably explains why, following that initial meeting, Livingston found himself chairman of the development committee which had voted unanimously to proceed as quickly as possible with the establishment of a Swansea branch. In due course, that chairmanship led to his election as the association's first president. The work flourished from the outset and, within a relatively short time, the new organisation became a reality and its headquarters were established in Herbert Place. Livingston found himself, with the considerable support of prominent church and chapel figures and colleagues from business, leading a vibrant organisation which was meeting the many challenges which stemmed from its objectives. Among those who worked with him from the earliest days were John Llewelyn, Charles Bath and Dr. John A. Rawlings, all of whom were associated with him in several other ventures. Rawlings and Llewelyn were, in due course, to succeed

Livingston as president, Llewelyn, who presided from 1908-27 becoming the longest-serving holder of that office. It was Livingston and his board, however, who laid the foundations for the activities of the association during the years of his presidency, and the pattern which emerged was typical of his thinking. Educational classes in a variety of subjects were offered, a debating society was formed, short-hand tuition was provided, Bible study groups were organised and a series of lectures arranged. In due course, because of the demand for seats, the Albert Hall was utilised for a series of evening events which combined popular entertainment with learned lectures and presentations which increased the knowledge and understanding of the audience in cultural activities such as music and art. The body was not forgotten in the planning of activities; football, cricket, gymnastics and other healthy pursuits, were on the agenda, while the spirit was the focus of the devotional meetings and the outreach mission work. For Livingston, the combination of activities which the YMCA could offer, the dedication of the leaders who had been appointed, the enthusiasm of those involved, and the obvious relish displayed by members and adherents for the many and varied activities which were on offer, were very satisfying. However, there were some dissidents. One group of young people complained that there were too many prayer meetings at the YMCA, and set up an alternative gymnastic organisation which was said to have flourished. Nonetheless, in the long run, it was the YMCA gymnasts, such as Arthur and Jack Whitford and Graham Harcourt, each of whom who represented Great Britain in Olympic Games, who between the twenties and fifties became famous outside Swansea as well as within.

So successful was Swansea's YMCA that, by 1881, it was necessary for them to move to new headquarters in Dynevor Place. Yet again, these premises were outgrown and, in 1911, the management committee obtained the freehold of the Longlands Hotel with a view to demolishing and replacing it with a new building which could meet the burgeoning demands being made upon the YMCA organisation in Swansea. That building still stands today at the corner of Page Street and St. Helen's Road, and may be regarded as a tribute to those Victorian pioneers who established the organisation in Swansea nearly 140 years ago. Those Edwardians who saw the need for, and raised the funds in such a short time to build a new facility which reflected the requirements of the twentieth century, should also be remembered.

The climax of the 12-day YMCA appeal campaign, 1911.

Whilst James Livingston did not live to see the new headquarters finished, he was involved in the planning discussions with the architect and builder regarding the various function rooms and associated facilities which would be included in the new structure. In addition, he helped to raise the funds which were necessary to allow this to happen. He and the architect who designed the building, Glendenning Moxham, were both at the public gathering to launch the fund-raising effort. During that meeting, the chairman of the new building committee, T. P. Cook, spoke of the growth of the organisation and of the part played by Councillor Livingston in ensuring its success. Cook reminded his audience that Livingston had been the first president of the Swansea association and that he still took an active part in its management. Subsequently, following 'a gloriously successful campaign', which lasted only twelve days, the handsome sum of £12,000 was raised to enable the building work to begin.[3]

At 80, Livingston was not actively engaged in the logistics of the fund-raising drive, but, he was able to offer his advice as to which people would subscribe significant sums. Sir John Llewelyn, who was president of Swansea YMCA at the time, was a natural target for an approach from Cook and Livingston. Llewelyn immediately agreed to pledge a four-figure sum, while Sir Alfred Mond offered to give ten per cent of the money subscribed during the next twelve days, and Roger Beck pledged five per cent. The most exciting part of the campaign, however, was the method used to reach ordinary people. George Rankin, who had secured substantial results in many parts of the country, and who was engaged to direct the campaign, advised that the immediate objective should be to raise £12,000 in twelve days. What attracted Livingston was the requirement for sixteen teams each of eleven members to 'forage' for pledges. The teams were all made up of young men with a Christian background and the elevens adopted names such as the 'Excelsiors,' the 'Hustlers' and the 'Try Hards'. Soon, the local papers reported, the town was 'on fire' and at the end of the twelfth day, in total the teams of young men had collected £3,054 to create a new record for such a task. Furthermore the 'Try Hards' also created one for a single team. Their total was £474, in which no sum was over £10, and 'very few at that.' The campaign director noted that the previous record had been held by Newport's young men, but no one had been as successful as had the Swansea teams. This involvement of ordinary people in the fund-raising process, not only resulted in an extremely useful contribution being made to the total, it ensured that the young people felt that they had played an important part of the process.

Livingston was delighted with the outcome and fascinated by the campaign masterminded by Rankin: weeks of planning, training the people who were going to canvass for the pledges, the acquisition of a poster site in the town centre, and the printing of a huge poster made up of 240 sections, which together made up a mural of the proposed building. As the pledges were registered, for every £50 obtained one of the sections was added to the mural. This gave the population a clear understanding of how much had been collected and there was great joy when Rankin scaled a very long ladder to put the last piece of the jigsaw into place. An item in the *YMCA Review* put the campaign into perspective when the anonymous writer commented that the people who had 'worked so hard to achieve the agreed objective should be conscious that their efforts would find permanent expression in the building that would stand . . . for generations to come'.[4]

REFERENCES

1. Quoted in: Farmer, op. cit., pp. 3 and 4.
2. Note the synergy between this concept and the Liberal ethic as described by Morgan, op. cit., p. 53: 'The Liberal ethic pre-supposed the harmony of classes, a cooperative ethic to unite middle-class enterprise and working-class solidarity.'
3. Anon: '£12,000 in Twelve Days', *The British and Colonial YMCA Review*, 1911, Vol. 5, No. 7, pp. 205-6.
4. Ibid., p. 2.

CHAPTER 7

Swansea Docks and the Chamber of Commerce

The keystone of Swansea's new harbour facility, the Prince of Wales Dock, was laid by Henry Hussey Vivian in April 1880. After the ceremony the dignitaries and other guests sat down to a 'sumptuous luncheon' which was followed by several speeches. By the time the Swansea MP rose to give his address the bottoms and minds of many of those present must have been somewhat numb. Furthermore, the numbness would not have been alleviated by Vivian's own speech, for he spoke for some twenty minutes, providing a mass of statistics in the process. It was true that the majority of luncheon guests had connections with the docks, but for many, the speech was something of a marathon. On the other hand, James Livingston listened attentively, for Vivian's discourse was supportive of his own ideas regarding the continuing development of Swansea's docks and the prosperity of the town. Indeed, it is highly likely that the two men would have discussed these matters over a long period of time. In effect, Vivian's theme was the need for Swansea to take advantage of its natural strengths and for it to develop an effective integrated system of supply: mine to railway – railway to docks – docks to vessel. Livingston had been arguing along these lines for many years, stressing the need for better rail links with the coalfields, particularly the Rhondda, more efficient traffic management, improved service to the vessels which took on cargo at Swansea, and the minimisation of charges like demurrage and pilotage. Since he was a coal exporter himself, there were those who viewed these activities as demonstrating self-interest. Whilst that was obviously true, as will be seen from the illustrations in this chapter, in working to improve the supply and handling system as a whole, he was benefiting everyone who used the facilities at the docks, presumably including his competitors. If that was self-interest, then it must have been of the enlightened variety.

At the luncheon, those who were able to maintain the necessary level of concentration would have found that Hussey Vivian's speech contained a telling illustration. Using Cardiff as a comparison, he told his audience that in 1840 Swansea shipped 500 tons of coal, whereas in the same year, only 166 tons were despatched from the eastern port. In the previous year (1879), 4,193,000 tons left Cardiff while Swansea's volume was less than twenty per cent of that total. They were striking statistics, which, according to Vivian, illustrated the vision of Lord Bute, who had recognised the importance of efficient docks and rail connections with the major steam coalfields. As a result, he had invested heavily in those facilities and 'the prosperity of Cardiff followed in its wake'. In effect, Bute's strategic awareness had virtually cornered the steam coal export market in logistic terms. In the process he and his allies more than compensated for the disadvantages from which the eastern town suffered as compared with Swansea. It was the illustration which Vivian used to demonstrate these disadvantages which caught the attention of many who might otherwise have nodded off.

Lundy Island, which the MP claimed was a useful reference point for making comparison, was fourteen nautical miles from Swansea. Bute Docks, Cardiff on the other hand was sixty-five miles away, and Newport a further ten miles to the east. This meant that a steamer passing Lundy, travelling at ten knots per hour, could be in Swansea about five hours before it could have arrived at Cardiff. He concluded his comparison by arguing that, taking tides into consideration, this enabled at least one-third of the vessels coming into Swansea to leave its docks well before the vessels which had sailed up to Cardiff or Newport. In addition, of course, the ships from the nearer eastern port would need to travel fifty-one miles further on their outward journey than those from Swansea. The question of why Cardiff, given its disadvantageous geographical position, was managing to ship so much more coal than Swansea, was the one which had been engaging James Livingston for some time. Hussey Vivian's parable and the theme of his speech brought the matter back into public focus. Livingston was to build upon that and upon his own forays which were intended to make the port of Swansea the most effective in south Wales.

In 1877, three years before Vivian made his speech, Livingston had chaired and addressed a special meeting of the Swansea Chamber of Commerce at the town's Guildhall. After quoting the tonnage figures for the harbour since 1852, he posed the question: Why are we lagging behind Cardiff? According to Livingston, one factor was the reputation of Swansea regarding mixing coals. He said that coals were mixed everywhere, indeed

Cardiff combined six tons for every one mixed at Swansea; the Cardiff people, however, were selling these coals as 'Powell Duffryn'. Next he questioned whether Swansea had within its reach steam coals of the quality then being shipped from Cardiff. If they could answer that question in the affirmative he believed that a significant increase in revenue for the port of Swansea would result. Livingston went on to argue that if there was a viable direct rail link between Swansea and the districts around Aberdare and Merthyr, this would make a major difference. He also pointed out that the best coal from these districts was nearer Swansea than Cardiff, but the mine-owners could get better rates per ton for shipping via the eastern port. In addition, the Cardiff line was direct, whereas that to Swansea involved changing tracks. Another area which needed careful attention, he believed, was the provision of facilities at the port to minimise the time taken to load and unload vessels. Livingston thought that unless the railways gave the mine-owners more competitive rates, or competition drove down costs while better facilities were provided at the port, then the mine-owners would continue to transact their business at Cardiff.

A further matter to consider was the activity of 'Cardiff merchants' who, according to Livingston, had 'spread misleading information about Swansea's facilities'. He had, he said, tried to establish a depot for Swansea coal in the Mediterranean, but found that there was a commonly held belief among the masters of steamers that Swansea coal was not suitable for their vessels, even though the product supplied was the same as that provided by Cardiff. His advice was that the foreign market should be 'flooded with circulars' giving the true information about Swansea, its docks and the products which were exported from there. Meanwhile, the Rhondda mine owners must be assured of adequate and competitive railway and port facilities so that they would not be disadvantaged were they to bring their business to Swansea.

A year later, in 1878, Livingston addressed another Chamber of Commerce meeting. This time he was campaigning for a reduction in harbour dues, 'to bring them into line with Cardiff and Newport'. He believed that, unless they were set at that level, 'the trade of the port will dwindle away'. According to a straw poll which he had conducted, the first question asked by the captains of vessels was 'What are you charging for port dues?' Yet, Livingston had cause to complain that one gentleman concerned with setting the level of these dues told him that 'it is not our

The Harbour Trust building, opened in 1903.

business to compete with Cardiff'. Nonetheless, building a new rail link between the Rhondda Valley and Swansea, would put 'within our reach' the whole of the output of supplies currently going to Cardiff'. However, in order to make inroads into that business, the charges levied at Swansea and the facilities and efficiency of the port must be competitive. He believed that in those circumstances the trade of the port would double itself in three years. As an illustration of the current disparity between the two ports, he quoted the case of a steamer captain who paid £20. 6*s.* 11*d.* at Cardiff, whilst a similar vessel was charged £28. 11*s.* 10*d.* at Swansea. He was convinced that fifty per cent of the Harbour Trust's membership were ignorant of these differences.

There were also other factors which affected the decision-making of ships' captains. He quoted a story that had been published in the *Cambrian* regarding a misleading pamphlet, which had been widely distributed by the Powell Duffryn Steam Coal Company. In it, the Cardiff firm had understated the depth of the water in Swansea harbour by more than three feet. The *Cambrian* comment on this information was that 'we have no right to infer that these gentlemen are dishonest, but it may serve their interests to deprecate Swansea in favour of Cardiff or Newport'. The irony in the comment spoke volumes about further dirty deeds in the east.

James Livingston had been campaigning on behalf of Swansea's business community since the early 1860s and, by the end of that decade he seemed to be on every major working party or committee. Sometimes he was the initiator of the task in hand; he often chaired meetings, and he was frequently a member of small groups which were sent as representatives of the Swansea business community to lobby on its behalf, or to press a case with decision-makers. In June 1869, for example, he was one of three people who 'waited upon the leading shippers, traders and tradesmen of the town and port' with respect to the additional rail services which were believed to be needed. Following these visits, Livingston and Lewis Llewelyn Dillwyn, the Swansea MP, travelled to London to present a memorial to the board of the Great Western Railway regarding these requirements. Unfortunately, the GWR directors would not agree to spend the the sum of between £40,000 and £45,000, which, they believed, was required in laying down track and providing the necessary equipment. Although he and Dillwyn were disappointed that they had not been successful, they were not downhearted. Given his fighting spirit, Livingston may well have muttered, under his breath, words about battles and wars.

At this point, it is interesting to note that, from the time he started to achieve a degree of standing among the town's business community, he attached great importance to serving his peers whenever the need arose. Since he was also associated with many other aspects of the life of the seaport town, one can only conclude that his business partners were extremely understanding, for he must have been absent from his office more often than not. Furthermore, as his reputation grew, his absences may have become more frequent, and he may have been away for longer periods. By 1873 his standing was such that in reporting a meeting of the Chamber of Commerce in September of that year, the *Cambrian* referred to his practical dynamism, calling him 'a man of action, not of words only'. The paper announced that Livingston was to coordinate a series of visits to interested railway companies with a view to improving services into Swansea. In his representative role he also travelled to Leeds two years later, along with Colonel Francis and a certain J. Mason. The task of the trio was to represent the Swansea chamber at a meeting of the Associated Chambers of Commerce which was being held in the Yorkshire city. Both the *Cambrian* and the *Leader* commented favourably on Livingston's performance. They reported that he had taken 'an active part in the discussion' and felt that he had done 'credit to himself and to the chamber which appointed him'.

A report in the *Mining Journal* of January 1876 also provides insight into Livingston's standing in Swansea and elsewhere. Discussing the construction of the Prince of Wales Dock near what is now Fabian Way, the journal stated 'the project has the hearty support of H. H. Vivian MP, Mr James Livingston [and others]'. The fact that the list ended 'with the powerful support of the GWR and the Midland Railway', is also noteworthy in assessing the man's perceived stature. Presumably, his persistence and persuasive powers had proved to be an effective combination yet again, at least as far as Brunel's railway was concerned. In June of the same year, whilst he was mayor of Swansea, Livingston received another accolade. He was installed as president of the town's Chamber of Commerce. As he was extremely conscientious and paid careful attention

Coal vessels waiting to load, Prince of Wales Dock, 1889.
(Gareth Mills Collection).

to all his tasks, that year, in particular, must have been one of the busiest of his life.

A year later, in 1877, Livingston addressed a special meeting of the Chamber of Commerce. His theme was the familiar one, this time entitled 'The trade of the port of Swansea', and, according to the *Cambrian*, he 'showed a complete grasp of the subject'. He told his audience that he had been involved with this trade for twenty-two years. Accepting this, it is interesting to know that he came into the business of exporting three years after the opening of the North Dock in 1852 and four years before the South Dock was opened in 1859. After a general introduction, similar to that given by Hussey Vivian three years later, Livingston addressed the question: Why is the port of Swansea lagging behind its eastern competitors? In summary, his conclusions were that the systems involved in moving coal from colliery to steamer for export via Swansea's docks were neither competitive nor effective. He stressed that the town had a 'magnificent dock, nearly complete, while the Harbour Trust is working to improve facilities for shipping by deepening the main channel'. Such action, he said, was essential, but without coal supplies of the right quality the dock would never be fully utilised. The development of the Rhondda and Swansea Bay Railway would be helpful in this regard, though it was pleasing to note that the GWR was now far more collaborative because 'they have very valuable wharfage, for which they have to pay a large annual rental'. He asked his audience to forget the previous disagreements with that company and to work with them to the best effect. There was a rider however, which was that 'we should refuse to countenance any scheme which would place in the hands of any one company the transportation of coal from a particular district leading to Swansea'. Livingston and Dillwyn might not have won the war with the GWR, but after losing the first battle they seem to have won the second. Furthermore, because the parties were now involved in a situation where there was mutual interest in the outcome, there was a genuine spirit of collaboration. This augured well for the provision of the improvements which Livingston had been advocating. In view of his comments on avoiding monopolistic rail-service providers, it must have given Livingston great pleasure, in due course, to see a new station (Victoria) opened near Burrows Lodge, for it was the site which he had favoured and one which would be serviced by a different railway company.

In September 1882, Livingston turned his attention to another weakness in the performance of the port of Swansea: bunkering. He reported to a Chamber of Commerce meeting that, 'within the last twelve months, 136 steamers in the North Dock could not take on bunker coal at the GWR tips'. This meant that either they had to wait or have fuel barged out to them, both of which added unnecessarily to the shipowners' costs. He said that the Harbour Trust and the GWR should ensure that additional facilities were provided so as to solve the problem. Then, repeating his familiar theme once more, he insisted that if the necessary action was not taken, Swansea would lose out to another port. During the same month, Livingston also became embroiled in a dispute between the Harbour Trust and the port's pilots and, subsequently, with the successful negotiations associated with the reopening of the station at Wind Street by the GWR. Among his other campaigns during this period was one designed to get members of the Chamber of Commerce to consider the longer-term impact on the town of the major decisions which they were taking. Though, in fairness to all managers/entrepreneurs of that era, the concepts and methodologies associated with long-range planning today had not been developed then. Furthermore, nor could they have conceived of the pace of change which would impact upon the business world within the next fifty years.

Livingston's next intervention was as a witness to the parliamentary committee, which was considering the Rhondda and Swansea Bay Railway (R & SBR) case. He argued that there were costly and inconvenient delays and frustrations in the existing system because it involved transferring traffic from one company's lines to another. Sometimes, he said, shippers were faced with delays of many hours, even whole days which, at the worst, could mean that a vessel might miss several tides, and always resulted in heavy demurrage charges. Indeed, such was the extent of the problem that it was almost impossible to overstate the potential savings involved. Livingston went on to press his case in support of the R & SBR option which, he believed was capable of bringing to Swansea 'not less than three million tons per annum'. That volume could not be achieved, however, without there being independent access to Swansea. Eventually, the bill was passed, enabling the company to proceed with their business, and Livingston had every right to feel proud of the contribution which he had made to ensuring that the planned railway became a reality.

In the late 1880s, when the authorities in Swansea were attempting to persuade the government to designate its port a harbour of refuge, Livingston seconded a Chamber of Commerce motion thanking the members of the delegation which had travelled to Bristol to attend a conference on the matter. He had recommended Mumbles Bay as being ideal for the purpose, but because such a development would result in the port enjoying a significant increase in its bunkering trade, interested parties representing Cardiff and Newport had opposed the motion. Unfortunately, the Swansea application was turned down. However, there was good news for the members of the chamber who attended that meeting, for they were informed that the volume of trade which was passing through the port was at a record level. It was announced that, during the first six months of 1888, shipments of coal had been 26,064 tons more than in the same period of the previous year. It was the best year the port had ever had and the total increase was 42,488 tons. All involved must have been delighted with the progress which had been made. If we are to judge by what the newspapers of the day reported, and the foregoing gives no more than an indication of what was published, then it is clear that James Livingston had played a key role the achievement of that record.

Paradoxically, as has been stated, his name is only mentioned in two of the books concerned with the history of Swansea.[1] This is surprising, for it seems evident that many of his contemporaries appreciated his abilities and his dedication to increasing the efficiency and well-being of the town's commercial life. Even at the age of seventy-four he gained sufficient support to be voted into office for the second time as president of the Swansea Chamber of Commerce. Some thought that the honour should have gone to a younger man, but Livingston took it all in his stride. For example, he was in the chair for a chamber meeting called to discuss whether they should go ahead with their traditional annual banquet. Some members felt that, unless they could be assured that an appropriate man of stature in the world of commerce would speak at the dinner, they should not proceed with the plan. In typical fashion, Livingston rallied his troops by providing a solution. He promised to contact Sir Alfred Jones, the president of the Liverpool chamber, and invite him to speak. Furthermore, he would 'put Sir Alfred up' and, as if to remind his colleagues that promoting a port was an ongoing task, he told them that, whilst the eminent Liverpudlian was in Swansea, Livingston would take him 'to see the site of the new dock to where he could send his steamers'.

Throughout his life, Livingston retained a concern for what was right and fair. For example, he believed implicitly in honesty in business and in treating people properly and with respect, whatever their station in life. In his early thirties, at a meeting of the Swansea Literary and Debating Society, he gave the vote of thanks following an address by Thomas Rees on 'Commerce'. Livingston said that honesty in business 'is a paramount essential of vital importance to trade.' In May 1891 he turned his attention to the conditions of service of Swansea shop assistants. Despite his position in Swansea society, he chaired a meeting at the Albert Hall called as part of a campaign for shorter hours. A year later, in supporting the Merchant Shipping Bill which the Liberal Party was promoting, he urged members of the shipping fraternity in the town, particularly the owners, to give greater consideration to their sailors. He believed that 'tens of thousands of seamen' had to live and work in substandard circumstances and that some owners exploited them.

One of James Livingston's last flourishes at a national level occurred when, as president of the Swansea chamber, he attended a meeting of the Associated Chambers of Commerce in the north of England. A major subject under discussion was a resolution for fiscal reform, and Livingston moved two amendments to the proposal. He contended that he wanted 'the matter to be taken out of party politics', which had 'a disturbing effect on commerce. We must get rid of it, not by a hybrid commission, which might well have personal interests to serve, but by a tribunal, fairly and honestly representative of all branches of commerce'. The amendment was lost by 40 votes to 39, but Livingston had shown, yet again, that his depth of knowledge, forceful personality, and his power as an orator were seemingly undiminished.

His final meeting as the president of the Swansea chamber, ended with 'a cordial vote of thanks to Mr Livingston for his highly appreciated service'. The speaker observed that 'the chamber has had some very good presidents but none superior to Mr Livingston'. However, if anyone thought that the patriarch would retire from business at that point in his life, they would have been mistaken. Two years later, he was still working both for his business and for his adopted town, for at a Chamber of Commerce meeting he made a presentation to E. P. Jones its secretary, in which Livingston was described as being 'the oldest trader in the port'. In reply, he talked about his earliest recollections of the port of Swansea. Enthusing as ever, he exclaimed, 'But, oh how marvellous has been the change . . . yet it is still in its infancy; there are great changes to come!' Delphi's oracle, it seems had nothing on James Livingston.

REFERENCE

1. See: Jones, op., cit:, p. 214, and Gerald Gabb, *Jubilee Swansea: The Town and Its People in the 1890's*. Vol. 2 [Swansea: The author], 1999, p. 96.

CHAPTER 8

Local Government

As will be clear to the reader from several sections of this book, James Livingston was a man who was inclined to take a firm stance on most topics. Certainly, he was unlikely to sit on the fence in any matter of importance. He was forthright, often with seemingly little concern for whatever others thought about what he said, and, in general, he maintained throughout whatever position he took at the outset. His position, *vis-à-vis* local politics, was that it should be free of national party allegiance. Thus, when he first stood as a candidate in the municipal elections, it was, in accordance with contemporary practice, simply as James Livingston, although it is fair to say that he was well-known as a 'Radical Liberal' in respect of national politics.

It was in 1869, when he was 38, that he entered local politics for the first time. In October of that year he attended a meeting at Swansea's Guildhall which was chaired by his old school friend, Thomas Cory. The

Swansea Town Council, 1911.
Livingston is seated on the extreme right of the front row with the 'boater' on his lap.

purpose of the meeting was to provide candidates who wished to represent the Lower Ward with the opportunity to express their views on local matters. On rising to speak, after being greeted by 'cheers and cries of bravo', he said that he was there because the present incumbent seemed to have done little or nothing. It appeared that 'a large number of Lower Ward people' were anxious that he should represent them on the council. Then, as the *Cambrian* reported: 'It is pretty well understood that he will be duly nominated'. No one doubted that he came to the contest with glowing credentials which were based upon both his wide-ranging activities in serving the town of Swansea, and upon his reputation as a business man and leading figure. Indeed, there could have been few that were not aware of his several achievements. Certainly, this was the view of the local press, the *Leader*, for example, stating that 'Mr Livingston has a deep interest in the progress and welfare of the town and port, is a thorough businessman and is altogether unswayed by anything like political bias and personal interest'. Had he written this tribute himself, Livingston would have been hard put to improve upon it as a testament to his standing. Then, as if to ensure that its readers were left in no doubt as to his qualities, the paper added, 'He would make a valuable adjunct to any council chamber'.

Even though his adoption as a candidate appeared to be a formality, Livingston left little to chance. As he had done before, he used the local press to communicate with the wider public. For those who had attended his adoption meeting, his letter to the *Cambrian* was a useful reminder of what he had said, whilst for those who had not, it was a clear statement of his philosophy as well as a reinforcement of his credentials. He wrote: 'At the earnest request of a large number of ratepayers, I offer myself as candidate . . . If you select me, my efforts will be directed without fear or favour, to the promotion of the interests of the borough'. Although his letter was, in part, a form of canvassing, he continued: 'I do not intend to canvas votes; firstly because I consider it wrong to do so, it being a reflection on the intelligence of burgesses; secondly because I have no time to devote to this purpose'. Presumably in case the last point in his letter might be misconstrued, Livingston felt it necessary to write again a week later. On this occasion he expressed his determination to devote whatever time was necessary faithfully to represent the interests of the ratepayers of Swansea. To underscore his approach to the task he concluded: 'I have neither private interest to serve nor party to represent!' Uncommitted readers in the Lower Ward must surely have been impressed by Livingston's approach. As many who knew him from his several activities in Swansea would have vouched, his philosophy was reflected in the way he acted as well as in what he said. He had other assets, too, which made him an even more appealing candidate; these were to be made apparent later in the campaign.

Although Livingston maintained his position on traditional canvassing, he could not avoid appearing in at least one election meeting. The event was held in a chapel hall in St. Thomas, and those who were there were treated to an explanation of his reasons for not canvassing. In keeping with his reputation for plain speaking, he lost little time in tweaking a nose or two as he developed his argument. He said that there were three classes of burgess in the town and he would explain his reasons for not canvassing any of them. Referring to the working class, he argued 'I know that they are not able to vote as they please', presumably referring to a common practice at the time, where large employers of labour put pressure on their workers to vote in a particular way. His reason for not approaching the second group – the middle class – was that, 'they know me well and are quite able to form an opinion of my fitness for office and are independent enough to act accordingly'. The third group – the large employers of labour – would not be canvassed by him, 'because I am determined that, if I went on the council, I will go unfettered . . . free to vote as I please, without the slightest feeling of obligation towards any person or party (applause)'.

It is likely that the aspersions cast in these statements, despite being framed in general terms, would not have been well received in several quarters. Consequently, this could have proved a risky tactic, for it might have been construed by some voters as indicating that he was so confident that he felt that he did not need to bother to canvas. However, if he had harboured such thoughts in advance of the meeting, the reception which he received at the end of the evening must have given him considerable reassurance. In terms of political risk, the positives easily outweighed the negatives. Yet that was simply one event: presumably Livingston would have needed to gauge reaction to the press reports of the St. Thomas meeting. Once again, his decision appeared to have been well-founded. His arguments looked good in print and, judging by the comments of the press and the outcome of the election, the majority of those who were not at the St. Thomas meeting also approved of the philosophies of this unusual man.

It could be argued that the key message which Livingston managed to communicate was that he was an independent, upright man of integrity: a powerful combination of assets for any would-be councillor. Yet that was not all he had to offer. At the end of his speech to the St. Thomas meeting, he told his audience that he had been 'looking closely' at the borough accounts, and he felt 'positively startled at the desperate state they were in'. He argued that Swansea was in the position of a trading firm whose receipts were not equal to its disbursements, whilst the burden of taxation was already too heavy. He went on to say that 'in the absence of some miraculous interference in their favour . . . it must swamp them!' In addition, he had identified a serious problem in the administration of the borough and, whilst he could not guarantee to put matters right, he would do all he could. Since the majority of his audience at St. Thomas, and of those who read about it, would not have been conversant with the vagaries of public and commercial accounting, the possibility of electing a man of integrity who was, obviously, experienced in dealing with such matters, must have been appealing.

When the votes were counted, Livingston's standing in the community, his personal qualities and his effective electioneering, proved to be enough to win him the Lower Ward seat. Interestingly, among those who voted for him were 'a large number of ladies', it being the first occasion that they were able to exercise their 'municipal rights'. There was also another intriguing aspect to this election. Notwithstanding Livingston's well-known anti-drink stance, both his nominator and seconder were involved in that trade: William Stone of the Mackworth Arms Hotel had proposed, and David Williams, wine merchant, had seconded. It would appear that Livingston's appeal as a prospective councillor was substantial enough to override other considerations, even if they might be potentially detrimental to business.

In typical fashion, on being elected, Livingston quickly became involved with the work of the council and in so doing demonstrated his business acumen through a number of early interventions. Initially, following up his remarks about the council's financial position, he argued for and achieved an extremely strict control on expenditure. Whilst these measures took some time to have any impact on the council's finances, Livingston's evocation of Mr Micawber's maxim served to help establish an ethos wherein those who were charged with spending the council's money did so with greater care. Furthermore, being aware that there was a continuing need to nurture and develop prudent attitudes, he took every opportunity to reinforce the message. For example, after his election, at a Ratepayers' meeting, he urged all present to support businesslike caution with regard to expenditure. His motto, 'No major expenditure until the deficit is corrected' proved to be a practical guideline for everyone involved in administering the business of Swansea Council. He remembered the pennies, too. Finding that some 'office personage' had bought an item of stationery from a London supplier when it could have been obtained locally, Livingston wanted an explanation. It was, he argued a matter of principle that 'public tenders should obtain the cheapest supplier in the trade'. In addition, everything else being equal, if possible the business should be given to a Swansea concern.

In October 1872, Livingston was continuing with his campaign to keep control of costs. He spoke in support of the mayor's unequivocal stance in refusing to countenance the level of stipend demanded by the magistrates for their new clerk. In his best 'They shall not pass' tone, he congratulated the First Citizen on preventing 'this great injustice to the people of Swansea (loud cheers)'. Since the magistrates had asked for double the amount proposed by the mayor, Livingston's assertion that their demand was 'most unreasonable and totally unmerited' was received by his audience with loud acclaim. Nonetheless, the matter was not resolved at that stage, and it was not until the following January that a compromise solution was reached. Then, in what the *Cambrian* called 'a very temperate speech' at a council meeting, Livingston set out to 'test the opinion of members on this *quaestio vexata*'. Whereas the magistrates had originally asked for £800 per annum and the mayor had suggested £300, Livingston said that 'it was useless to kick against the prick' because the magistrates 'hold the upper hand', and recommended that the sum of £500 be the annual stipend for the clerk. Presumably, he had taken the matter as far as he could without endangering the service which the clerk's office provided for the town. He might not have won the battle, but it was clear that he had not lost it either.

James Livingston became mayor of Swansea at an extremely important time in the development of the town and port. One of his earliest tasks was to have the council agree to proceed with the proposed new docks scheme. Everyone was aware of the position he took on the matter, and whilst Livingston was confident of obtaining the necessary support, there were those who dissented. The new mayor, however, started with the advantage that, with his Chamber of Commerce hat on, he had been a prime mover in conceiving of the need for the new facility, as well as in the planning from which the proposal arose. Not surprisingly, having contributed so much to the preliminary stages he was anxious to see the matter resolved in line with the proposal. He believed that it was of considerable gravity, an opinion with which the *Cambrian* agreed. Indeed, in March 1876 when Livingston called a special meeting to discuss the issues involved, the paper called it 'undoubtedly the most important that has ever taken place in the history of Swansea'. Then, later in the item, the paper referred to the 'unprecedented magnitude' of the decision with regard to the commerce of the town and port. Not that Livingston was at all fazed by the paper's opinions. He was certain that it was the right decision for the port and town of Swansea to proceed with the scheme. Despite the opposition of his old adversary, James Rogers, the mayor carried the meeting with him; the proposal of the Harbour Trust was heartily endorsed. Furthermore, when the electors were consulted on the matter any remnants of opposition were swept away by the 'unanimous and enthusiastic' response of those who attended the meeting. Five months later, the Swansea Harbour Act of 1876 was given royal assent and work began on the project shortly afterwards. As the future was to show, the *Cambrian*'s assessment of the importance of the decision which Livingston had driven through was to be validated. It was, indeed, a momentous achievement.

In passing, it is interesting to note that Livingston was the first mayor to wear the new chain of office, which had been presented to the town by his friend Frank Ash Yeo, who had preceded him in the office.[1] On donning the chain he said that he considered it a great honour to be the first to wear the magnificent gift and that he would endeavour to make himself worthy of it. At the end of his term of office as mayor in November 1876, the *Cambria Daily Leader* paid tribute to Livingston. In the opinion of the paper, the retiring mayor had discharged his duties for several years efficiently and effectively. In addition, he had 'fought well and persistently for the establishments of the new docks, upon which the future prosperity of the town so much depends'. In responding, Livingston was expansive in his gratitude to all those who had worked closely with him during his mayorality. He said that he had tried to do his duty to the best of his ability and supposed that the people had cooperated with him because they 'saw that I have tried to do what I could in the interests of Swansea (cheers)'. The objective observer would have found it difficult to disagree with that statement, for from the moment he was elected as a councillor he had played a leading role in the management of the affairs of the town and port.

Whilst he ceased to act as mayor, Livingston continued to play a key role in managing the affairs of the town and port. For example, a year later, in 1877, he negotiated on behalf of the council with the representatives of the board of the Swansea Improvements and Tramways Company, namely, Charles Bath, chairman, and Francis Heseltine. Bath and Livingston knew each other very well, having worked together in conjunction with the Harbour Trust. It is fair to say that both men were dedicated to ensuring the welfare of Swansea, but, Bath, of course, had a major responsibility to his shareholders. To put the negotiation into context it would be helpful here to outline the background to the discussions which took place in the council offices.

The passing of the Transport Act of 1870 had a considerable impact upon the development of street tramways throughout the United Kingdom. With its population increasing at a significant rate, Swansea did not wish to be left behind in the matter of public transport. Consequently, specialist surveyors were employed to report on the feasibility of a suitable tramway system for the town. Unfortunately, the resulting report stated that many of the town's streets were too narrow to enable a tramway to operate effectively. With the need for public transport increasing, the promoters of the original scheme regrouped, and in 1873 put forward a further proposal which was to make Swansea unique in the way in which tramways were provided. The Memorandum of Association in describing the object of the new company included, of course, the application to Parliament to carry out the scheme for the construction of tramways. What made it unique was the associated aim, 'to effect certain street and other improvements in the town and port of Swansea'. The scheme was received with enthusiasm, and in June 1874 royal assent was given for it to proceed.[2] Not only was the act unique in including the improvements provision, the same was true insofar as it necessitated a public-private collaboration for which there was no precedent. The act authorised the corporation to

An illustration of the narrow streets which were one of the problems facing the contractors in developing the tramway system in Swansea.

An early tram near the Cameron Arms Hotel.

appoint a tramways committee to oversee the making of appropriate financial contributions towards the cost of improving streets, demolishing unwanted buildings and widening key highways. Obviously, the broad agreement outlined in the act necessitated careful negotiation of specific arrangements. For example, what proportion of the costs involved would be met by either party? When would the system be active? Which routes would be developed first? Which street improvements should be given priority? Livingston's discussions with Bath and his colleagues were undertaken against this background, although, nearly three years after the passing of the act, the development of the tramway system had been subject to numerous delays, partially through the withdrawal of several contractors in succession. Both parties were frustrated, and what the *Cambrian* called a 'furious row' erupted when the tramways company announced plans to extend its line from High Street to Cwmbwrla Square. Initially, the corporation refused to sanction these plans because the company had not completed all the improvements which had been promised within the time specified by the act of Parliament. While Livingston was well aware of the financial pressures bearing down upon the company, his position was simple: the improvements which had been promised should be completed first. On the other hand, the company needed to increase its income stream in order to be able to undertake the improvements. After several meetings the parties agreed to a compromise. The plain fact was that the tramway company's commercial considerations were the key to providing the solution which the negotiators eventually found. Even that success did not mark the end of the problems which arose as the public-private partnership was brought about. Nevertheless, having in mind that Livingston and Bath had to satisfy ratepayers and shareholders, the importance of those negotiations with respect to the eventually successful development of Swansea's tramway system cannot be overstated.

Despite the completion of his term of office as mayor, Livingston's influence on leadership and key decision-making regarding the business of the town and port of Swansea continued to be significant. By then, he had established a reputation as an able, trustworthy, business-oriented councillor and was a member of a number of committees. In addition, he was never afraid to introduce ideas, which he saw as being beneficial to the town and port, even if they were controversial. He argued, for example, that the Harbour Trust and the corporation were essentially one, that their interests were identical; and the sole object of both bodies would be the good of the town. He believed that the two should merge, resulting in an organisation which was logically sound; something which could not be said about the then current arrangements. Livingston, who served both organisations, claimed that several advantages would arise from the new organisation. He argued, for example, that there would be significant savings on staff costs, alone, for he believed that £2,000 to £3,000 per annum would accrue from an amalgamation, while £6,000 could be saved each year on interest by consolidating Trust borrowings with those of the council. After demonstrating how these benefits might be achieved, he went on to say that he had been 'credibly informed' that the arrangement which he suggested was perfectly feasible and would receive the immediate sanction of Parliament. He was certain, too, that the bondholders would welcome the proposed change. Unfortunately, influential people in both organisations thought otherwise, so Livingston's idea never came to fruition.

At this distance, given the obvious benefits of the suggestion, and there is no record of the arguments of those who opposed the idea, one can only assume that, in his enthusiasm for the project and for its potential benefits for Swansea, he did not give adequate attention to the 'diplomatic' work which is necessary when human nature is involved. The desire of key office holders in each organisation to retain their positions in the *status quo*, for example, is perfectly understandable. Yet, presumably, Livingston did not take sufficient account of that fact. From his perspective, all that mattered was that Swansea would benefit if the idea was taken up. Perhaps his myopia in the matter suggests that the former mayor found it difficult to accept that diplomacy is an important element in the armour of what we would call today, a 'change agent'. Yet, if confronted by that argument, he could have pointed to numerous examples where, despite ignoring such matters, he had successfully brought about change.

James Livingston served Swansea as a councillor for more than a decade before reverting to his business and to the many organisations with which he was involved. However, in 1902, at the age of 71, it was reported that he wanted to return to the council chamber. His desire did not please everyone; some believed that he was too old for the task, while other opponents said that he would be relying on a 'sympathy vote' in order to get elected. Whether that was true or not is impossible to say, though, after learning so much about the man, to us it hardly seems likely. Suffice to say that he was again victorious and, with his talents being well-recognised in council circles, he was quickly elected to several committees, including that concerned with the town's tramways system. Not that this stopped him from being his old beligerent self. At the beginning of 1905, under the headline 'Breeze at Guildhall', it was reported that there had been a contretemps at a committee meeting concerned with the town's 'dust distructor'. Livingston wanted to know if it would 'pay its way', in response to which the chairman argued that it was 'never envisaged that it would make a profit'. Typically, Livingston would not let go of the bone. Presumably, in an effort to defuse what was proving to be a heated argument, several members suggested that a subcommittee, including Livingston, be formed to examine the issues. The age old ploy of setting up a subcommittee whenever a difficult situation arose seemed to have lowered the temperature, but the chairman, probably irked by Livingston's stance, could not resist saying, 'I hope that Mr Livingston will come with a view to assisting rather than obstructing'. Hackles raised again, the former mayor responded with a tirade which left no one in doubt that he was there on behalf of the ratepayers and would not be fobbed off. He had a similar problem with Alderman Tutton with whom he clashed in another committee. Thereafter, the alderman found it difficult to work with him. Presumably, the patriarch was not satisfied with taking a back seat and Tutton and certain other incumbent leaders may have seen him as a dinosaur sent back to try them. Nonetheless, Livingston remained as focussed as ever. As he said after one committee room fracas, 'I am here to carry out my special mission'. Friends and enemies knew what he meant by that: he was there to look after the interests of the port and town of Swansea. In fairness, though, on occasions there were those who, whilst not necessarily objecting to his statements, disliked the way he went about achieving his objectives.

Nonetheless, whilst he had some problems with the diplomatic side of his work, given his age, there were very few people with the quality of his experience and expertise, not to mention its longevity. In consequence, when the incoming mayor proposed that a special asylum committee be formed, Livingston, who had seconded the motion, was appointed chairman, despite the opposition of his *bête noire*, Tutton. As the future was to show, he and his committee were to do sterling work in difficult circumstances to set up a facility which in itself was not exactly high on

A Bert Thomas cartoon published during the local authority election of 1907 showing Livingston's reaction to the boasts of the other Party.

the popular appeal scale.³ Nevertheless, in September 1907 Livingston was still fighting to establish the asylum, and he used the local election of that time to press his case in human and economic terms as a benefit for the town. Several sites had been considered as being suitable for the purpose, including Fairwood Common, Clyne Common, and Cefn Coed. However, there were several objectors to the Fairwood and Clyne suggestions, notably from the Commons and Footpaths Preservation Society, following which it appeared that Cefn Coed, Swansea, would be selected. Nevertheless, it was not until 1 April 1908 that the matter was finalised and negotiations with the owner of the land concluded. In the meantime, Livingston had been successful in his negotiations with Merthyr, for that town was to have a one third share in the operation of the asylum. Whilst the joint scheme did not come to fruition during Livingston's lifetime, it is interesting to note that days before his death in 1912, he was re-elected to the chair of the asylum committee for another term. Another achievement for the patriarch.

It was in the same election campaign, that James Livingston gave his audience another insight into the inner man. At a Victoria Ward meeting when he was somewhat incensed by a verbal attack from one of his opponents, he declared with a mixture of pride and agitation: 'There'd have been no Prince of Wales Dock if Mr Yeo and myself had not spent three of the best years of our lives struggling for it!' No one came forward to refute that claim. Then, in another meeting, he showed that he had more insight than the average man about himself, at least if measured against Burns's 'To see oursels as ithers see us'. He told his audience that forty-five years had passed since his first election speech, and 'if there is a stubborn, independent, pig-headed man in Swansea, I am that man (applause)'. He went on to reaffirm his independent stance, declaring, 'I do not follow anybody unless my conscience and judgement go with them'. Whatever his shortcomings, his personal profile still proved to be attractive to the ratepayers; he defeated Captain Bradford by 606 votes to 508, which did not please his opponent. In a tetchy post-election interview, the captain said that supporters on both sides admit that Mr Livingston secured 'numbers of votes out of sympathy'. There was a rider, too; it appeared that this was especially true of widows. Presumably, since Livingston was 76 at the time, one can assume that the ladies proffered their votes purely on their democratic judgement. After all, the patriarch had been a widower for thirty years or so and was hardly a matinee idol.

REFERENCES

1. See: J. R. Alban, 'The Guildhall, Swansea', 1984, Swansea City Council and George Grant Francis, *Notes on a Gold Chain of Office*. Swansea Council, 1876. Frank Ash Yeo, who was mayor immediately before Livingston, commisioned the chain. George Grant Francis had been asked by Yeo to produce a specification, agree it with him and with the goldsmith involved and to liaise with the latter throughout manufacture. On taking office and being first to wear the chain, Livingston asked Grant Francis to produce an explanatory booklet about the chain, its design and its heraldic interpretation. This was published in 1876 and contained a dedication to Livingston.
2. The Swansea Improvements and Tramways Company Ltd Act (1874). The company agreed *inter alia* to 'making of new streets, the laying down of tramways'.

3. Following the passing of the Lunacy Act, 1890, there was a requirement for each county in the UK to build its own psychiatric hospital – then called lunatic asylums – and to do so within a given period. For various reasons the town council did not meet the scheduled dates, but had an interim arrangement with Glamorgan County Council with whom they shared a facility at Bridgend. This contract was terminated in 1904, when a new agreement was made which lasted until 1909. During this period, an arrangement was made to share the planned facility with Merthyr, and in 1910 a joint committee was set up, with Cefn Coed, Swansea being the agreed site. The 1914-18 war intervened, and foundations were not laid until 1917. Thereafter, because the money was not available, Swansea Council was unable to build the hospital for many years. Indeed, it was not until 1932 that Cefn Coed Hospital was finally opened. By then the agreement with Merthyr had lapsed.

CHAPTER 9

Further Activities

The earlier chapters in this book have focused on particular aspects of the life and times of James Livingston. Here, the intention is to consider some of his other activities with the objective of adding to our understanding of this extraordinary man. As information was gathered during the research stage, it became clearer that he must have had an amazing amount of energy and that his was a dedicated commitment to any task which he undertook. As has been demonstrated, he adopted a 'hands-on' approach to the management of particular projects at the start-up stage and, then tended to delegate leadership to other able men. Given his multitude of activities, that made a great deal of sense. On the other hand, there are examples of lifelong service, such as his various roles in the Wesleyan Methodist Church, his work for the temperance movement, his activities in association with the Chamber of Commerce, and his dedication to Swansea Cricket and Football Club. If he were to have refused any offices beyond these no one could have complained, for there must have been few gaps in his diary, even when only these activities are taken into consideration. Yet, as will be seen from this chapter, whenever there was a worthy cause, Livingston was to the fore.

For example, in January 1869 he became a trustee of Swansea Savings Bank and an evening manager.[1] Twelve months later, at the company's annual meeting, the chairman, Hussey Vivian, spoke warmly of Livingston and thanked him for his work for the bank. In August of the following year, he demonstrated his willingness to work for the benefit of the whole of the business community in Swansea when he, John Richardson, Charles Bath and Thomas Cory formed a committee to consider the installation of telegraphic news facilities in the town and port. Taking account of the names of the other members of the group, his inclusion in it is indicative of his standing in Swansea's business community, and in 1871 this was endorsed by his appointment to Swansea's Board of Guardians. Furthermore, together with Charles Bath, he attended a meeting of the Cambrian Rowing Club, which is indicative of his love for sport. He told his audience that, whilst he was not an active member (he only subscribed to their funds), his sympathies were entirely with the club. He would always, he said, recommend that young men took up healthy active pursuits.

On the business front, in October 1873 Livingston and Thomas Cory registered the Swansea Ship Owning Company Ltd., the purpose of which was to purchase and work steam and sailing ships. Such was the standing of the partners that, at the time of the announcement, £40,000 had already been subscribed. Three years later, Livingston chaired several meetings of the Ship Owners and Brokers Association, which is another example of his standing in the town and of his resolve to help improve the efficiency and effectiveness of the port of Swansea.

Livingston's involvement in local politics is discussed in Chapter 8, but it is interesting to examine here a case in which he was an innovator and when he demonstrated, once again, his inclination to tell all, as he saw it, in the interests of what he believed to be right. In March 1883 Livingston presided at a meeting at Holy Trinity Schoolroom, the particular purpose of which was to analyse the burgess roll as a means of identifying eligible temperance voters, so as to ensure that all anti-drink candidates could be given every support. This information was used in preparing for the election, but as the voting day approached, personalities were cited and the temperature of the contest rose quickly. Typically, Livingston was prepared to put his head up over the parapet and say what he thought should be said. At a meeting in Madoc Street Chapel in support of Thomas Trew and Albert Mason, he claimed that an opposing candidate, John Glasbrook, had suggested a reduction in the wages of council workmen whilst raising the salaries of the 'higher levels'. This, he said, was typical of the approach of the owner of Morriston Colliery: putting the poorest at the disadvantage. The colliery owner was swift with his reply. Writing to the *Leader* he denied saying any such thing. 'I advocated,' he wrote, 'the adjustment of labourers' wages. Many get into the council employ by favour and get the same wages as hardworking men, although some of them are butlers and not fit for hard work.' Difficult as it is to see the connection between manservants and grace-and-favour employment, it would not have been hard to respond with Professor Joad's observation: It all depends what you mean by 'adjustment'. Livingston, however, largely ignored the opportunity to reply in print. Instead, he challenged Glasbrook to a public debate with an audience of South Ward voters. This seems to have caught the attention of the public, because a number of correspondents wrote to both Swansea papers. Indeed, judging by one letter, from a certain Abram Francis, there was a public appetite for such a contest. He wrote: 'Both men are able to deal with local questions – Mr Glasbrook, with his keen wit and accustomed shrewdness and Mr Livingston with his well-known eloquence'. Other letters followed, one of which was from Livingston. The election had been popularised as the Brewers versus the Temperance Men, with John Glasbrook being cast as an agent of the former group. For Livingston this meant that his own candidate's opponent was fair game for straightforward exposure. In his letter he pointed out that the Morriston colliery owner had claimed to have paid a significant amount in council charges. Livingston said that he had checked and found that Glasbrook had paid £15.15s when he ought to have been charged at least £200. Unfortunately for Livingston, though, his letter and his innovative use of the electoral roll did not have the desired effect: John Glasbrook, supported by the licensed victuallers emerged as victor. Interestingly, despite the bad feeling which this exchange engendered, when John Glasbrook died in April 1887, Livingston attended his funeral. Does that, one might wonder, tell us something more about our subject? Had he turned the other cheek? Or had they found some common ground from which to work together?

In line with Livingston's philosophy about parties and local politics, that election had not been fought on a Liberal ticket, but he was well-known as a member of that party. Indeed, when the new Liberal Club was opened in Swansea in 1885, his portrait was hung alongside those of Sir Hussey Vivian and Robert Burnie, the MPs. In the following year that recognition took a tangible form when he was elected to the general committee of the club. Thereafter, in particular, when national Liberal policies were involved and local action was necessary in support, Livingston's presence was guaranteed

One of the items in the Queen's Speech for 1880 was concerned with the government of Ireland. The Liberal Party was in favour of change, and it was not surprising that James Livingston should throw his hat into the ring and assist with the campaign in support of that objective. For him, the Irish tenant farmers were another group of disadvantaged people who needed help. Furthermore, as he saw it, the actions of the representatives of the Establishment were exacerbating the horror of the situation, and Livingston had tilted at that particular windmill on many occasions. It may seem strange at this distance that there should be enthusiasm in Swansea for Irish Home Rule, yet the concept of 'distributing' land more equitably had its supporters in the town as it had elsewhere in the United Kingdom. The idea of landed gentry was beginning to be challenged and land reform was a popular topic with the masses, though there was little focus at the time on home rule for Wales.

The campaign in Swansea for Irish Home Rule was well received, and thousands turned out to listen to and cheer the speakers who were making that case. In April 1886, for example, a meeting was held by the Liberals to give the people the opportunity to hear about the government's current thinking on the matter. Lewis Llewelyn Dillwyn was the speaker, with Livingston in support. In the following month, the Liberals arranged an open-air meeting in a field near the Compass Inn in Cwmbwrla. Standing on a wagonette, Robert Burnie and Livingston spoke to an enthusiastic crowd, with the latter being buoyed up by the atmosphere generated by the enthusiasm of the audience. When he rose to speak, he could not resist the temptation to ridicule a political opponent. In the course of presenting the resolution to support Mr Dillwyn and Mr Gladstone in their efforts to deal with the Irish problem fairly, with the betterment of the Irish people in mind, he referred to Sir John Jones Jenkins, who 'was frequently in a political fog, (roars of laughter)'. He finished his speech with a clarion call to put the needs of the Irish people before those of the grasping absentee landlords.

In May 1886, Livingston returned to the anti-aristocratic mode which he had adopted in a letter to the *Leader* in October of the previous year. In that letter he suggested that the emoluments and salaries which the aristocracy received from the public purse were far greater than the taxes which they paid. He called this a 'gigantic system of outdoor relief for the aristocracy of Great Britain', and included a list of dukes, marquises, earls, viscounts and barons who benefited from this national largesse. His purpose in making this revelation was, he argued, to support Gladstone and his leading colleagues in bringing contentment and peace to the Irish people. Livingston was not alone in taking this position and, in 1888, in recognition of the support of the local men, Gladstone came to Swansea, to be met at High Street Station by a party of local Liberal leaders, including Livingston.

No doubt, Gladstone was aware of the campaign which had progressed so favourably in Swansea, and which was typified by another open air meeting at Dyfatty Fields at the beginning of 1887. The burden of the argument presented on that occasion by Livingston and Burnie was embodied in the resolution which the thousand-strong audience enthusiastically endorsed: 'This meeting is of the opinion that the Irish Coercion Bill, rushed through by an unscrupulous Tory government is being promoted not to suppress crime, but to deprive Ireland of its political and social rights.'

Livingston continued with this theme in a letter to the *Leader*. His muse must have taken fire, for he wrote: 'In this supreme moment of our national life, we have resolved that Ireland shall at last have justice and freedom. It is important to bear in mind that Landlordism and Shylockism are the curse of that unhappy country'. After referring again, to the absentee landlords among the aristocracy he turned to what he called 'the fighting landlords'. These were the military men who held property in the country. There were, it seemed, two generals, thirty-one colonels and fifty middle-ranking officers. By his action, Livingston demonstrated, yet again, that he was prepared to tilt at the most powerful windmills. Certainly, his stance could hardly have endeared him to one of the most influential groups of people in Britain. Interestingly, following Livingston's letter, Frank Ash Yeo, MP, Livingston's friend and fellow Wesleyan, an Englishman by birth, made public the fact that he looked forward to home rule for Scotland and Wales.

Livingston, of course, was not in a position to influence decisions at Westminster. Quite rightly, he saw his role as supporting whoever represented Swansea Liberals in Parliament, as well as Gladstone and his cabinet. Nonetheless, his favourite area of activity was in local politics and government, because he believed that he could bring to bear greater influence at that level ,whilst being able to convert talk into action. He liked to see tangible results and, indeed, his reputation in Swansea had been built upon making things happen. In 1887 he was a key speaker at Calfaria Baptist Chapel, Ravenhill, when the meeting declared itself in favour of the disestablishment of the Church in the principality.[2] No doubt, Livingston had in mind his own experience with the Church and its tithes, but his objective on this occasion must have been to support the official Liberal line on the matter. As it happened, action did follow words: the Anglican Church in Wales did become disestablished, although, as a result of the onset of the 1914-18 war, the passing of the act was delayed until 1920.[3]

In the meantime, Livingston continued to use his best endeavours to influence and support matters which were of concern to him. Sport and healthy activity were very much on his agenda and in May and September of 1888, he was one of the judges at swimming galas at Swansea Baths. The second of these events was held under the patronage of John Llewelyn (knighted in 1890), his friend and colleague in several of his activities, but a political opponent. Not that the friendship deterred Livingston from making rather frank statements when he thought such comments were justified. One which would not have endeared him to Llewelyn, was his assertion that 'Sir John, a Tory MP, is not a free man. He is tethered head and foot to a policy which he does not believe. He is helpless, and Swansea does not want a helpless representative in London.' The objective reader would probably argue that the party system placed the majority of MPs in that position. In any event, John Llewelyn did not have a long tenure as an MP in Parliament. At the 1900 election the Swansea knight was ejected in favour of Sir George Newnes. Wrapped up in that victory was another controversy involving Livingston.

On 12 October the *Leader* published its opinion repudiating the suggestion that Livingston had staged a demonstration at a rugby match in favour of Newnes. The incident occurred at St. Helen's on the Saturday before voting took place. The All Whites were playing Plymouth, an extremely attractive fixture, and Newnes, Swansea's Liberal candidate, made it known that he would like to see the match. After stating that Newnes's opponents would never believe that the incident was unplanned, the paper's leader writer went on to argue:

> And yet he [Livingston] had no more to do with it than the veryest man in the street. Swansea's representative is a keen lover of football, but, because of his engagements at open-air meetings, he was unable to be at St. Helen's Field until about a quarter of an hour after the kick-off. At that point Mr Livingston, quite properly, escorted Sir George and Lady Newnes to the grandstand. What else would his opponents have him do?

Following a heated aside, Sir George's advice to Livingston was 'I would suggest that you do not allow the utterly false and unworthy implication to annoy you'. Whilst heeding this advice, Livingston must have pondered over his wide-ranging network of activities and relationships. With respect to the incident, for example, Newnes' opponent was Sir John Llewelyn, the president of the Swansea club, Livingston was vice-president, and both were trustees of the St. Helen's lease. Obviously, it would have been extremely difficult for Llewelyn to escort his opponent to the grandstand. Yet, for Livingston, there must have been a moment when he wondered how people could put such an interpretation on the incident. But then, to rephrase the old saw, 'all's fair in love and politics'. Not all those opponents who had suffered from his verbal or written barbs would have turned the other cheek.

At sixty-nine, in the year 1900, Livingston showed little sign of slowing down. He continued to participate in his many fields of activity as well as appearing in others. In June he was the starter at a charity athletics event, and he performed the same duties at the Swansea Grammar School sports later in the year. Wearing his Chamber of Commerce hat, he became involved, from the outset, with the fight to rescind the Coal Tax Bill. As a member of the Chamber's Emergency Committee, and with his encyclopaedic knowledge of shipping coal, he was in an ideal position to help influence matters. Among other things, he produced telling statistics demonstrating that the port of Swansea had already lost a significant tonnage as a result of the imposition of the tax. He forecast that the export market for British coal would be decimated if the tax was not removed. In due course the government changed its position and Livingston and his colleagues who had fought against the tax, must have felt very pleased with their efforts.

Soon after Alderman Thomas of Lan's death in January 1909, Livingston became one of the members of a committee set up to decide upon a suitable memorial to the champion of the open spaces. This was appropriate, if only on the grounds that Livingston and Sir John Llewelyn had worked closely with Thomas during the fight to save St. Helen's from the developers. At the first meeting, it was decided that a statue should be erected in the town as a permanent reminder of the wonderful legacy which had been left to its people as a direct result of Thomas's campaigns. Livingston proposed that a 'shilling fund' be set up to raise the sum necessary to erect the statue. Not surprisingly, the fund flourished and, within weeks, the committee put the contract out for tender. The two most attractive quotations received were shortlisted. Each of the would-be contractors had submitted a design and, at first, the committee was divided as to which to select. Each party made a presentation, during which they were asked to name the sculptor who would be involved in the work. One of these, from William Brown (who had been successful with his tender for the Boer War memorial) stated that the work would be undertaken in Liverpool. As a result, it was the second offer which was selected. Appropriately the successful bid was tendered by another Swansea man, Ivor J. Thomas. What swayed the committee was Livingston's recommendation that a local artist who would do the work in Swansea would have the benefit of understanding the background and have greater feeling for the commission. Livingston also had another motive. As he had advocated many years before, he believed in Swansea's economy benefiting wherever possible as a result of the council purchasing its needs locally. While that decision was made without acrimony, Livingston, taking a typically obdurate stance, argued against siting the Thomas of Lan statue in Victoria Park. He believed that it should be erected in the town and not in the park, where the Boer War memorial had been placed two years earlier. Despite his strong support for the concept of the statue, he felt that putting it up in an open space was an 'act of vandalism'. This, however, was a minority view and, at the end of July 1906, following a short ceremony, members of the public as well as dignitaries witnessed the monument being erected in the park. While Livingston did not have his way on this occasion, his stance may have influenced a subsequent decision by the council to resite the Boer War memorial. Perhaps the decision-makers thought that two memorials in the same park was not entirely appropriate.

At seventy-four, Livingston was still ruffling aristocratic feathers. In November 1905 he made a powerful speech in the council chamber regarding the ownership of land. Against a background of significant unemployment, he put forward a proposal which, he believed would help alleviate the poverty and misery being faced by those without work. In his opinion, the ownership of vast areas of land by a small number of individual landlords was a 'flagrantly unjust principle'. He wanted local authorities, wherever there was concern about the disadvantaged, to have the power to purchase land at a price which 'gave a reasonable margin for the tillers of the soil'. He spoke about Garibaldi's success in 'liberating' land in Italy and of the benefits that it brought. In typical fashion he cited examples of landowners making vast sums of money out of letting their land for shooting parties, when some might be used for productive purposes. At one point, with his muse on fire, he declared that, on behalf of the disadvantaged, he would 'take the stand in a revolution tomorrow'. His rallying call was 'You shall not keep the land for deer or game reserves, and let us go starving!' This was the compassionate Livingston with his heart on his sleeve, whose judgement in public discourse was sometimes coloured by his concern for his fellow man. Not surprisingly, his detractors seized upon the hyperbole, accused him of being a communist, and wondered whether they might help themselves to some of his coal? However, time was to show that the fundamental issue upon which his argument was based reflected an underlying trend which would result in a significant change in land ownership in fewer than two decades.[4]

REFERENCES

1. When the Swansea Savings Bank was established, one of the problems which faced the organisers was the need to gain the confidence of working-class savers in the bank. Few, if any, of these people had experience of banking and thus needed reassurance that their money would be safe in the hands of those who ran the business. Since working men could only visit the bank after finishing their shift, it opened its doors during certain evenings. The role of the board members who also served as evening managers was to oversee the activities, ensure security, and help give depositors confidence in the banking process by their presence and through answering questions raised.
2. A Baptist chapel might appear to be an unusual venue for a discussion about the disestablishment of the Anglican Church in Wales. In the late 1880s however, the Baptists and other nonconformist chapels were strongly in favour of the concept and they had a powerful voice at Westminster: Lloyd George was a Welsh Baptist.
3. The Welsh Disestablishment Act (1920).
4. As Morgan records, op. cit., p. 186. 'In Wales, the years between 1918 and 1922 were to see the most dramatic phase in the process of land transfer. In this period more than a quarter of the land of Wales changed hands'.

Epilogue

When writing a biography, at the research stage an author may turn to a variety of sources of information. For example, in some cases there may exist an archive of the private papers of the person concerned, or those of people or organisations with whom he or she was friendly, or with which he or she had worked. In the case of James Livingston, however, the main source proved to be the local newspapers of his day, augmented by some archive material from Swansea Cricket and Football club, the YMCA, and from the Swansea and Gower Methodist Circuit. Unfortunately, several of the other organisations with which he was involved during his life in Swansea lost their records during the Second World War air raids on the town, or as a result of lack of interest in preserving them. Fortunately for the authors, the contemporary newspapers, which are available, provided us with a rich seam of information, which, on reflection, is not surprising, for James Livingston maintained a high profile in Swansea over nearly four decades. He was a colourful character who wore his heart on his sleeve, a man who took a single-minded approach in dealing with business, social, educational, sporting and spiritual matters, and for whom the inter-relationship between each of these activities was seamless. The same basic set of beliefs were the foundation for his interventions in each and every sector of his life.

In addition to being a successful businessman, he was an extremely able speaker with a commanding presence, and yet he remained a compassionate man with a selfless approach to life. As will have been seen from the foregoing chapters, time and again he showed concern for the welfare of his adopted town and its more disadvantaged citizens. He gave himself wholeheartedly to public service for the betterment of Swansea, and was a key figure in the planning and development of several projects which, history was to show, made a significant contribution to the effectiveness of the town and port. That he could be obstinate, blunt and, sometimes, less than concerned about the viewpoints and feelings of those who opposed him concerning whatever he saw as the right way to approach a problem, cannot be denied. Certainly, he did not court popularity; indeed, in making some interventions, particularly with regard to the Establishment, he attracted hostile opposition which could not have been to his advantage.

As the reader will be aware, one of Livingston's major activities during his lifetime in Swansea was his association with Wesley Chapel. He served the Wesleyans in many ways, one of which was as superintendent of the Sunday school. Unfortunately, the detailed records of both the chapel and its schools were lost during the blitz on Swansea, and we have had to gather whatever information was available from secondary sources. Happily, though, the transcript of a talk given in 1893 by a man who had been a pupil at the school in the mid-1860s was brought to our notice. Apart from providing us with an intriguing picture of the school itself and some of its scholars, it enhances our understanding of the remarkable James Livingston. As indicated earlier (see p. 53) the transcripts of William Robinson's lecture paints a picture of a challenging social community within which the school's teachers and leaders strove to educate young, disadvantaged people in a Christian environment. That work was part of an ongoing mission to bring such people, particularly the young, into the church family. As was seen in Chapter 5, by the time described by Robinson, Livingston had established himself as a major figure in this work, and the lecturer's comments indicate something of the bond which was developed between the young scholars and their teacher. Robinson wrote, 'He was our Livingstone, and in our young days we associated him with the idea of true bravery, indeed we thought him like Garibaldi in his appearance . . . certainly equally as brave, but a kinder-hearted man by far. In fact, the biggest part of this big man seemed to be his heart'.[1] Livingston, then thirty years of age, had obviously made a deep impression on the young man, one which, judging by the tone of his paper, was unchanged thirty years after the event.

Comments which were made when Livingston was appointed to 'the high and honourate office of chief magistrate' in November 1875, provide a further, broader-based insight into our understanding of the subject of this biography. His sponsor, Alderman Ford, said of the new mayor: 'Mr Livingston has been the architect of his own fortune and, in the conduct of his life and important business . . . he has given the best proof of his business qualifications'. After recording the fact that he had brought, and would continue to bring these talents to bear in the management of council affairs, the alderman went on to comment on Livingston's personal standing. He declared that the mayor's moral character stood forth predominantly, and in the interests of the burgesses of Swansea he had been 'found to be foremost'. Then, in conjunction with the Masons, Oddfellows, Foresters and the charities of the town, and everything that would 'tend to be to the advantage of the inhabitants of the borough, he has always been in front (hear, hear)'. In saying this, the alderman stressed that he was merely reporting the facts, which his own experience of working with the new mayor had shown to be true. This tribute was then reinforced by the example of the council's accounts which Livingston had brought 'out of chaos when he came to the board'. Turning to Livingston's other characteristics, Ford gave it as his opinion that an effective chairman ought to be a popular man, 'who endeared himself to his fellow burgesses by contributing to their comfort and advantage'. The alderman had no doubt that the new mayor 'has brought forward the amelioration of the condition of the masses of Swansea . . . and also that he has opened his purse to every movement of the kind'. Thus he met that criterion.

It is probably true that the tribute to an incoming mayor would tend to focus on his strengths rather than weaknesses. Nonetheless, after being immersed in the story of James Livingston for almost three years of research and writing, in our view what was said about the new incumbent in the foregoing paragraph and elsewhere in this text, is entirely justified. If any doubts exist in the reader's mind, they will be removed by the eulogy published in the *Cambria Daily Leader* on his death, which will put the mayoral tributes into a broader perspective, and which helps support our contention. The fact that Livingston's passing was given such space in the paper (and similarly in the *Cambrian*, and *South Wales Daily Post*) is indicative of the nature of his standing in the community. The opening sentences of the *Leader* tribute, which are reproduced on the back cover of this book, are illustrative of this. After stressing that he leaves a void which may never be filled, the paper went on to note that Livingston had been in business in Swansea for over fifty years, and that few men were better known, and

. . . none more generally appreciated both for sterling character and all-round capabilities . . . He, with Mr Frank Ash Yeo was among the few who fought a terrific battle for the Prince of Wales Dock. To this there was great opposition and a town's meeting was called . . . The Livingston-Yeo party won. As a Mason, too, he had a brilliant career; he was a member of Caradoc Lodge and held most offices in Freemasonry.

That he was much travelled and fluent in French provided the focus for a further section in the eulogy, much being made of the scope of his business connections abroad. The fact that Livingston had been aboard the first train to enter Paris following the end of the Franco-Prussian war in 1871 was cited as indicating his energetic approach to selling. Another of what were described as his 'adventures' occurred when he was arrested on suspicion of being a spy, which gave a hint of his aura of bravery that had been noted by his Sunday school pupil. Apparently, the arrest was due to a misunderstanding, the authorities being cautious about a block of 'evil-smelling patent fuel which was included in his baggage'

The reference to Livingston's 'brilliant career in Freemasonry' provides yet another facet of his abilities and standing. A founder member of Caradoc Lodge, he was senior warden in his first year. He became Worshipful Master of that lodge in 1877, an honour which the *Leader* believed he had 'gained worthily'. Then, in March two years later, after performing the ceremonial relating to the installation of a new master 'with Masonic perfection', he 'received the commendation of the lodge' and was presented with a pastmaster's jewel together with 'every expression of appreciation as to the marked ability with which he fulfilled his duties'. As if to confirm the validity of that tribute, the chairman of the event announced that Livingston was one of just two people 'elected to serve on the Provincial Grand Committee'. Then, in March 1881 he became a member of the Past Provincial Grand Lodge. Whatever his detractors might have said, these appointments may be seen to be indicative of the perceived qualities of a remarkable man who, in many different spheres of activity, was propelled into senior positions of responsibility within relatively short periods of joining an organisation. To have achieved such recognition so quickly in so many different cases suggests that James Livingston must have been an outstanding personality and a formidable, personable, skilful and effective leader of men. He must have looked the part, too. In 1897, when he gave evidence at the House of Lords to a Parliamentary select committee regarding Swansea's Tramways Bill, he was addressed twice as 'Sir James'.

Despite this, it should be recognised that throughout his time in influential positions in Swansea organisations, notwithstanding his many successes, he had his detractors. Some of these were clergymen in the Established or Catholic churches; others were political opponents, a number even from his own party, or, in the context of his work with the Welsh Rugby Union, from other towns. One common characteristic at the root of his relationships with most of these detractors, was Livingston's tendency to speak his mind and to refuse to budge from the position which he had taken. There were few shades of grey in his approach to any matter of concern to the community; with him it was either black or white. One is left to wonder whether he might have been even more successful as, what is termed today, a 'change agent', had he been more diplomatic and taken greater trouble to understand the other party's position. That, of course, can only be left to conjecture, as indeed must be the mystery surrounding the fact that this remarkable man has previously attracted so little attention in publications relating to the history of the town and port of Swansea. It is hoped that the latter omission will be satisfied to some degree by the present publication. At least, readers of this book will know something about Livingston's life of service, a benefit previously denied to those interested in learning more about the people of Swansea in Victorian and Edwardian times.

In the spring of 1906, when the *Cambria Daily Leader* published a series of 'Sketches of new JPs', Livingston, who was 75 at the time, joined the bench at Swansea. The paper, noting his age, said of him: 'Councillor Livingston is the "youthful patriarch" . . . Although upward of the allotted span, he takes a keen interest in movements athletic, and for years has been a prominent member of Swansea Cricket and Football Club . . . and he has travelled much on the continent. He possesses strong feelings, but has good judgement. Councillor Livingston was mayor in 1875 and is the current president of the Chamber of Commerce'.

In closing this final chapter of this book, we have to acknowledge that we set out to be objective about James Livingston. We knew very little about him, but as our study and subsequent writing have evolved, we have come to admire our subject greatly. Apart from his many achievements, his seemingly unbounded energy, his dedication to innumerable causes and his personal qualities, he achieved so much despite personal tragedy. He outlived two wives and lost his youngest daughter when she was only twenty-three years of age. Lesser men might not have continued to live a life of selfless service to God, to their town and to those who lived within its boundaries. Few would have had the physical, mental and spiritual strength to continue undaunted. But then, Livingston always acknowledged the origins of his strengths.

One of the documents which we obtained early in our research, was a copy of Livingston's will. This simple record provides further evidence of the man's values. Although he was a successful businessman, merchant, shipowner and man of property, his total estate, according to the *Calendar of Wills*, was valued at only £2,100.15s.4d. Whilst it is true that such a sum was worth far more in 1912 than it is today, one might have expected such a well-connected senior businessman to be far richer. Presumably, this outcome is indicative of a generous, selfless man whose orientation had little to do with acquiring money for its own sake. It certainly seems to confirm many of the observations which are made in this book, and the assumptions upon which they are based.

REFERENCE

1. Robinson, op. cit.

Bibliography

BOOKS

Alban, J. R. (1984) *The Guildhall Swansea: Essays to Commemorate the Fiftieth Anniversary of its Opening*. Swansea City Council.

Baxter, T. P. (1970) *The Port of Swansea*. University of Manchester BA Hons thesis. Swansea Institute.

Beynon, David H. (1994) *Swansea's Street Tramways: The Story of Swansea Improvements and Tramways Company Limited*. Swansea Maritime and Industrial Museum.

Briggs, Asa (1996) *Victorian People: A Reassessment of Persons and Themes, 1851-67*. London: Oldhams, 1954; Rev. ed. Chicago: University of Chicago Press (1970).

Davies, T. G. (1982) *A History of Cefn Coed*. Swansea: West Glamorgan Health Authority.

Davies, T. G. (1995) *Guide to the Committees of the County Borough of Swansea*: Swansea City Council.

Farmer, David (1995) *The All Whites: The Life and Times of Swansea RFC*. Swansea: DFPS.

Francis, George Grant (1976) *Notes on a Gold Chain of Office, Presented to the Corporation of Swansea in the Year 1975*. Swansea City Council.

Gabb, Gerald (1995) *Jubilee Swansea: The Town and Its Peoples in the 1890s*. Vol. 2 [Swansea; The author], 1999.

Griffiths, T. Gwyn, (1985) *Garibaldi, Cymru Fydd a Dante*. [Swansea]; Coleg y Brifysgol, Abertawe.

Harris, Edward (1934) *Swansea: A Brief History*. Cardiff. Western Mail & Echo.

Hughes, Stephen (2000) *Copperopolis: Landscapes of the Early Industrial Period in Swansea*. Aberystwyth: The Royal Commission on the Ancient and Historic Monuments of Wales.

Jones, W. H. (1995) *History of the Port of Swansea*, Carmarthen: Spurrell, 1922; Facsim. ed. [Swansea]. West Glamorgan Archive Service.

Lambert, W. R. (1983) *Drink & Sobriety in Victorian Wales*. Cardiff: University of Wales Press.

Morgan, Kenneth O. (1981) *Rebirth of a Nation: Wales, 1880-1980*. Oxford: Clarendon Press; Cardiff: University of Wales Press.

Neilson, Grenville P. (1983) *Swansea's Wesley Chapel: The Story from John Wesley's Visit to its Destruction*. Ilford: Odcombe.
Owen, J. Alun (1995) *Swansea's Earliest Open Spaces: A Study of Swansea's Parks and Their Promoters in Nineteenth Century*. Swansea: Swansea City Council.
Rogers, W. C. (1981) *A Pictorial History of Swansea*. Llandysul: Gomer Press.
Williams, Glanmor (Ed.) (1990) *Swansea: An Illustrated History*. Swansea: Christopher Davies.
Williams, Stewart (1975) *Vintage Buses and Trams in South Wales*, Barry: The Editor.

ARTICLES, PAPERS

Anon. '£12,000 in Twelve Days', *British and Commonwealth. YMCA Review*, Vol. 5, No. 7, July 1911.
Jones, E. W. (1910) 'Recollections of Twenty Years of South Wales Cricket', in *St. Paul's Church Sketty: A Souvenir*. Sketty Church, 1910; Facsim. ed., Swansea: City and County of Swansea Library and Information Service, 1999, pp. 50-2.
Livingston, J. (1910) 'Football', in *St. Paul's Church*, Sketty, supra, pp. 22-4.
Meers, P. D. (1986) 'Yellow Fever in Swansea, 1865'. *The Journal of Hygiene*, Vol. 97, pp. 185-91.
Neilson, Grenville (2000) 'Dr. John Adams Rawlings (1848-1933). *Minerva*, Vol. 8, pp. 27-36.
Richards, S. (1976) 'The Rhondda & Swansea Bay Railway'. Typescript.

OTHER RECORDS

Caradoc Lodge of the Freemasons archive
County Borough of Swansea. Asylum Committee book, 1906-11
The Swansea & Gower Wesleyan Church archive
Swansea Chamber of Commerce. *Minute Book*, 1884-88
Swansea Cricket Club. *Minute Book*, 1866-1871

NEWSPAPERS CONSULTED

The *Aberystwyth Observer.*
The *Cambria Daily Leader.*
The *Cambrian.*
Mumbles Press.
The *South Wales Critic.*
The *South Wales Daily Post.*
The *Swansea Gazette & Daily Shipping Record.*

DIRECTORIES (Where the title varies by edition, the latest is cited.)

Bath, T. E. *The Excelsior Guide to Swansea and the Mumbles*, Swansea 1880.
British Association for the Advancement of Science, Swansea, 1880. *The Official Guide and Handbook to Swansea and Its District* . . . Prepared . . . by S. C. Gamwell. Printed at the *Cambrian*, Swansea 1880.
Butcher's Swansea and District Directory: . . . London: Butcher & Co., 1875, 3rd edition, 1881.
Kelly's Directory of the Principal Towns and Places of South Wales. London, 1891.
Lewis, John. *The Swansea Guide.* Swansea; Brewster, 1851; Facsim. ed. [Swansea]: West Glamorgan County Council Library and Information Service, 1989.
Mercer & Crocker's Directory for the Counties of Glamorganshire and Gloucestershire, Leicester: 1876.
Pearce's and Brown's Swansea Directory, Swansea: 1869.
Slater's Directory of Gloucester . . . Hereford . . . and . . . South Wales. London: 1868 Manchester: 1880.
Swansea and District Trades Directory, Swansea: Printed at the *Cambria Daily Leader*, 1902.
Woods, John Chapman. *A Complete and Reliable Guide to Swansea and the Mumbles, Gower*, London: Simpkin, Marshall, 1883.
Worrall's Directory of South Wales. Oldham: 1875.
Wright's Swansea and Mumbles Guide. Swansea: 1906.

Index

Aberdare, Lord, 60
Aberystwyth Observer, 26
Albert Hall, 48, 66, 79
Alexandra Road, 65
All France XV, 39
All Whites, 38, 39, 40, 100
Anglican Church (see also Church of England), 46, 99
Army of Right, 44, 49
Ash-Yeo, Frank, 12, 29, 31, 52, 86, 93, 99, 107
Associated Chambers of Commerce, 75, 79

Bancroft, Billy, 34
Band of Hope, 45
Barbarians, 40
Bath, Charles, 65, 87, 89, 95, 96
Beck, Roger, 68
Blue Ribbon Movement, 45, 47
Blue Ribbon Choir, 47
Blue Ribbon Savings Bank, 37
Board of Health, 19
Boer War memorial, 102
Bowen, William, 38
Bradford, Capt., 93
Brewer, Mary Jane, 19, 52
Briggs, Prof. Asa, 14
Bright, John, 21
Brown, William, 102
Brynmill Terrace, 34
Brunswick Chapel, 53, 54, 58, 59
Brunswick Chapel Choir, 56
Bryn-y-môr Field, 34, 35, 62
Burnie, Robert, 97
Burns, Robert, 93
Burrows Lodge, 19, 20, 76
Buse, J W, 62

Bute Docks, 71
Bute, Lord, 71

Calendar of Wills, 109
Calfaria Baptist Chapel, 99
Cambria Daily Leader, 12, 15, 23, 33, 38, 56, 75, 82, 86, 96, 98, 100, 106, 107, 108
Cambrian, 21, 23, 27, 28, 29, 30, 33, 34, 35, 42, 48, 60, 62, 73, 74, 75, 76, 82, 85, 86, 89, 106
Cambrian Rowing Club, 96
Capel Als, 21
Catholic Church, 46, 108
Caradoc Lodge, Freemasons, 107
Cardiff, 71, 72, 73, 74, 78
Cefn Coed, 92
Charles Street Congregational Church, 56
Church of England, 21, 26, 27, 28, 32
Churchill, Lord Randolph, 47
Church rates, 20
Church of Rome (see also Catholic Church), 26, 27, 28
Cleveland Terrace, 19, 52
Clyne Common, 92
Coal Tax Bill, 101
Commons and Footpaths Preservation Society, 92
Cook, T P, 67, 68
Cory, Thomas, 16, 52, 81, 95, 96
Cwmbwrla Square, 89

David, Thomas, 46
Dillwyn Llewelyn, John, 15
Dillwyn, Lewis Llewelyn, 47, 48, 74, 76, 98
Dissenters, 21, 47, 48
Dissenting Chapels, 44, 46

Dyfatty Fields, 99
Dynevor Place, 66

Education Act of 1902, 31
Established Church (see also Church of England), 108

Fairwood Common, 92
Ffynone House, 58
Ford, Alderman, 105
Forrester, Charles, 33
Foresters, 106
Francis, Colonel, 74
Freemasons, 106, 107

Garibaldi, Guiseppe, 55, 102
Gladstone, William, 98, 99
Glamorgan Cricket Club, 37
Glasbrook, John, 96, 97
Goat Street, 19, 25, 28, 45, 46, 58
Gorse Lane, 34
Gospel Temperance Union, 45, 48
Gower and Swansea Wesleyan Methodist Circuit, 59
Grace, W G, 36
Great Ridbaxton, 53
Great Western Railway, 74, 75, 76
Grenfells, 49
Guildhall, Swansea, 46, 49, 71, 81

Harbour Trust, 4, 73, 89
Harcourt, Graham, 66
Herbert Place, 65
Heseltine, Francis, 87
High Street, 64, 89
High Street Station, 98
Holy Trinity schoolroom, 96
House of Lords, 108

Irish Home Rule, 98

James brothers, 39, 41
James, Evan, 41
Joad, Professor, 96
Jones, Sir Alfred, 78
Jones, E P, 79

Jones, E W, 35
Jones, W H, 12, 14
Jones-Jenkins, Sir John, 98

Landore, 30
Latch, Amelia, 55
Leisure Centre, 19
Lewis, J, 45
Liberal Party, 46, 47, 97, 98, 99
Liberal Club, 97
Lillywhite, 36
Liquor party, 47
Livingston, Beatrice, 53
Livingston, Earnest, 53
Livingston Ethelwin, 53, 57
Livingston, Frank, 56
Livingston, Burton, 56
Livingston, Irene, 53
Livingston, Mary Jane, 53
Livingston, William, 16
Llewelyn, John (also as Sir John), 11, 20, 34, 35, 36, 40, 49, 64, 65, 66, 68, 100, 101
Llandeilo, 43
Local Option, 46, 47
Longlands Hotel, 66
Lower Ward, 82, 83, 84
Lundy Island, 71

Mackworth Hotel, 38, 84
Madoc Street Chapel, 96
Madrid, 30
Mansel Street, 53
Mason, Albert, 96
Mason, J, 74
Mayor of Swansea, 52, 108
McCutcheon, W, 41
Merchant Shipping Bill, 79
Meredyth, W H, 47, 48
Methodism, 53
Methodist Church, 45
Metropole Hotel, 40
Micawber, Mr, 84
Midland Railway, 75
Milan, 30
Mining Journal, 75

INDEX

Mond, Sir Alfred, 68
Monte Carlo, 31
Morgan, Colonel, 35
Morgan, Kenneth O, 44, 46, 50
Morriston Colliery, 96, 97
Mount Street, 19
Mumbles Methodist Church, 56, 59
Mumbles Road, 34

Nantmelin Colliery, 19
Naples, 30
Neilson, Grenville, 55
Newnes, Sir George, 100, 101
Newnes, Lady, 100
Newport (Mon.), 68, 71, 74, 78
Nonconformist, 27
   (see also dissenters)
Northern Union, 38, 39, 41
North Dock, 41, 76, 77

Oddfellows, 106
Olympic Games, 64, 66
O'Shanter, Tam, 28
Oxford Street School, 31, 32

Page Street, 66
Paris, 39
Penlle'r-gaer, 64
Perkins, C H, 40
Plymouth Rugby Club, 100
Powell Dyffryn, 72, 73
Prince of Wales Dock, 70, 93, 107
Pugh, Mrs, 34

Queen's Speech, 97

Ragged School, 49
Rankin, George, 68
Rawlings, Dr John Adams, 47, 48, 50, 52, 59, 65
Rees, Rev. David, 21
Rees, Thomas, 79
Rhondda, 70
Rhondda & Swansea Bay Railway, 76, 77
Richards and Livingston, 19, 53
Richardson, John, 95

Richardson family, 29
Robinson, William, 54, 55, 105

Salvation Army, 47
Second World War, 104
Sketty Debating & Drama Society, 27
Sketty Methodist Church, 59
Smiles, Samuel, 63
Smoking, 37, 38
South Dock, 20, 76
South Wales Football Cup, 64
South Wales Daily Post, 106
Spoforth, 36
Squires, Rev. E B, 21, 22
St. Helen's (Field), 11, 15, 36, 37, 39, 41, 62, 100, 101
St. Helen's Road, 66
St. Helen's lease, 101
St. Helen's Workingmen's Club, 29
St. Thomas, 83, 84
Stone, William, 84

Sunday School, 52, 55, 58
Swansea:
  – Bay, 30
  – Board of Guardians, 95
  – Chamber of Commerce, 11, 12, 17, 71, 72, 74, 75, 76, 77, 78, 79, 86, 95, 101, 108
  – C of C Emergency Committee, 101
  – Cricket Club, 11, 33
  – Cricket & Football Club, 36, 41, 42, 62, 95, 104, 108
  – Cricket League, 43
  – Debating Society, 29
  – & Gower Wesleyan Record, 53, 57
  – Harbour Act 1876, 81
  – Hospital, 53
  – Improvement & Tramways Company, 87
  – Literary & Debating Society, 29, 31, 79
  – Rugby Club, 11, 39, 64
  – Savings Bank, 95
  – Schools League (Rugby), 41
  – Ship Owners & Brokers Association, 96

115

- Ship Owning Company, 96
- Workingmen's Club, 11, 25, 29, 43, 60, 61, 62, 64, 65
- YMCA, 25, 29, 43, 56, 65, 66, 67, 68, 104

Temperence, 44
Temperence Party, 47
Thomas, Ivor J, 101
Thomas, William of Lan, 11, 15, 35, 36, 101, 102
Tithes, 21
Tithe Rent Charge Act 1891, 23
Tucker, John, 36
Trew, Thomas, 96
Tutton, Alderman, 91

Unitarian Church, 60
Uplands Hotel, 62

Vance, Rev. G H, 60, 62
Victoria Park, 102
Victoria Station, 76

Victoria Ward, 91
Vivian, Henry Hussey, 70, 71, 75, 76, 95, 97

Welsh Liberals, 26
Welsh Sunday Closing Act 1881, 50
Wesley, John, 16
Wesleyans, 26, 52, 53, 55, 60, 95, 99, 105
Wesley Chapel, Swansea, 19, 25, 27, 45, 53, 54, 55, 57, 59, 105
Wesleyan Home Mission, 56
Wesleyan Foreign Mission, 56
Welsh Rugby Football Union, 11, 42, 108
Whitford, Arthur, 66
Whitford, Jack, 66
Williams, David, 84
Williams, E G, 23
Williams, Prof. Sir Glanmor, 14

Yellow fever, 20
York Street Chapel, 29
YMCA Review, British and colonial, 69